WITCH'S MAGICKAL SPELLBOOK

Witch's Magickal Spellbook

Transform common plants into tools
for love, luck, and renewal

Priestess Moon

ROCKPOOL

A Rockpool book
PO Box 252
Summer Hill
NSW 2130
Australia

rockpoolpublishing.com
Follow us! rockpoolpublishing
Tag your images with #rockpoolpublishing

ISBN: 9781923208988

Published in 2026 by Rockpool Publishing

Other images: Shutterstock
Design and typesetting by Sara Lindberg, Rockpool Publishing
Edited by Lisa Macken

Caution: always check with your medical practitioner before using any herb if you are pregnant, breastfeeding, or have a medical condition.

A catalogue record for this book is available from the National Library of Australia

Printed and bound in China
10 9 8 7 6 5 4 3 2 1

This grimoire belongs to:

____

Contents

Introduction

The *Witch's Magickal Spellbook* is a recipe book of enchanted spells and potions that explores the world of kitchen witch magick. Within this book you will learn to craft simple charms and magickal potions by using common kitchen ingredients such as herbs, spices, fruit, oils, and salts, which most people have on hand or can easily source, to shift and shape energy.

This is an interactive book you can use to write, spell craft, color in, journal, and cook, using the stickers provided to seal your charms with extra enchantment. You can even eat some of your spells!

The enchantments in this book use the concept of sympathetic magick, which is magick that involves using objects you have an affinity or connection with in rituals to create a desired outcome. Certain objects will have stronger cultural connotations for certain qualities; for example, those with European ancestry generally associate roses with love, gold coins with wealth, four-leaf clovers with luck, and white feathers with angelic messages.

Sympathetic magick is not a new concept: humans have practiced it for thousands of years, and it is often referred to as folk or tribal magick. This kind of magick considers the spiritual or metaphysical properties of natural objects such as plants, flowers, and crystals. It is believed that every living item has an energetic blueprint and certain items resonate with certain energies; for example, rose quartz crystal is believed to hold an energetic resonance that opens your heart chakra and brings about love and healing.

Performing a spell is a creative way to focus on positive intent, and engaging in prayer, rituals, or spell work can have a profound effect on your brain. The neural networks in your brain form paths, or highways,

depending on the thoughts you focus on. The thoughts you have repeatedly are the ones that become dominant in your brain, with the neurons creating thicker networks for the electrical thought impulses to travel along. Thinking in a catastrophic manner or, alternatively, thinking in a positive manner, becomes habit.

It is absolutely possible to change your thought patterns, with research indicating that with practice changes occur at a chemical level. This is known as neuroplasticity. When you create an enchantment with confidence and a playful spirit you do more than just engage in positive thinking: you actively bring forth the realization of your highest hopes. This approach not only empowers you, but it also nurtures a joyful mindset that can lead to positive outcomes. By using intention and focus, along with a practical approach to refining your attention, spell crafting can become a valuable tool for a better life.

Use the hashtag #witchsmagickalspellbook on Instagram to show me your creations, as I would love to see your experiments! I have tried and tested all the recipes in this book, but if you have tweaked any of the recipes to make them better I would really enjoy hearing about that too and will look forward to giving your version a try.

How I learned to work with energy

At the age of 10 I wrote a book called "Witch's Magical Spells." It contained a variety of charms written in the style of cooking recipes, complete with illustrations and lashings of sequins and glitter. I made potions in the garden with leaves, flowers, and dirt, stirring the ingredients with a wooden spoon in my mom's old saucepan and chanting made-up magickal words. You could say my curiosity about spell work and herbal recipes started quite early!

Fast forward 10 years and I'd completed my Bachelor of Arts in Design and decided to travel to Scotland to discover the land of my ancestors. I'm Australian but my heritage is Scottish and Irish and I resonate with my Celtic ancestry, which is why most of my artworks are heavily influenced by illuminated manuscripts such as the Book of Kells.

My last name is Fraser, and part of my family is originally from the Scottish Highlands. My Scottish heritage is the clan of the Lovat Frasers, who were involved in the battle of Culloden. If you've even watched the series *Outlander*, the main character Jamie Fraser is a Lovat Fraser and our family motto is "*Je suis prest*," which means "I am ready" in old French. Culloden Battlefield has an eerie feeling to it, and when I visited I found the whole place quite overwhelming.

Before I arrived in Scotland I wondered if I might find grand castles and surprise treasures, but instead I found myths and legends about fairies and nature spirits and a rich thread of folk magick and ancient rituals running through the modern highland culture that was fascinating.

I spent a lot of time walking through forests, running around standing stones, and performing spells and rituals with herbs and plants and stones, and it just seemed so natural to me. I researched more into the Druids and Celts spiritual practices and even tried to learn Gaelic!

In Scotland I found a strong link between nature and spirituality, the sacredness of trees and woodlands and a respect for the divine beings that control the natural world. This nature-based spirituality comes through in all of my work. I was intrigued by how food and drink were used in Highland magick and ritual; for example, when drinking whisky a special cup, the quaich, is used when welcoming guests and friends at weddings to symbolize love and friendship. Another delightful thing I learned is that food is often left out for house spirits known as brownies.

I visited Ireland as well, another part of my family history, and discovered the triple spiral at the Neolithic site of Newgrange, which is my sacred symbol and one I have tattooed on my left arm. I found that spending time alone in nature surrounded by trees and standing stones and creating rituals using rocks, plants, and flowers so peaceful and healing that I knew this was the perfect way to express my spirituality.

The whole concept this book is based on is the idea that on an energetic level plants contain metaphysical and spiritual properties that attract certain qualities such as love, luck, and protection into your life.

What is a kitchen witch?

I practice kitchen witch magick. For those of you who are unsure about what a kitchen witch is, it's a person who uses cooking ingredients to create magick. The spiritual properties of plants and minerals are all pressed into service to create spells and potions. I like to rummage about in my pantry and find ordinary items such as potatoes or toothpicks to create fun recipes and rituals.

A kitchen witch focuses on seeing the ordinary as well as the divine as being sacred. This involves honouring the goddess by taking care of hearth and home, blessing daily household tasks, and observing the solstices and equinoxes. Ideally, everyday cooking is imbibed with light and magick, although I'd like to point out that this is not always possible but it's good to have a life goal!

The magical uses of all plants in this book are my own interpretation, through practice and influenced by the spell and plants books referenced in the bibliography.

Working with the fae

When you work with plant magic and the natural world you cannot help but come across faery energy. The fae are the guardians of the natural world. This elemental energy is within the forces of nature: fire, earth, air, and water. In European folklore fire fae are salamanders, earth fae are gnomes, air fae are sylphs, and water fae are undines. You can work with this energy in your spiritual practice: see the Protection chapter beginning on page 109.

Luck has long been associated with the faery folk, in the form of bestowing magickal favor upon humans. My understanding of a faery is that the fae were a race that once lived on earth in physical form and were bonded with nature in a very real way. They could talk to trees and plants and find healing cures, they were and still are intuitive, magickal, and telepathic, and they are incredible artists and craftspeople.

It is believed the fae now live in a parallel dimension, a band of energy that is a different frequency from our current physical world. The fae are like us: they have good souls, cheeky souls that are still evolving, so that's why some like to help humans and others like to frighten them. When humans continue to clear forests and natural landscapes for profit it is a repugnant practice to them.

As a child I'd always been fascinated with faeries, and when I moved to Scotland at the age of 21 I was actively seeking the faery folk. This was the land of my ancestors, where the myths and legends I'd read about had come from, and with a little practice and patience I began to feel their presence, their otherness. They were gentle, playful, powerful, mischievous, and curious about humans. I tapped into fae energy and cultivated a deep respect for and working relationship with the fae. My belief had morphed from an intellectual one into a heartfelt one.

Craigmonie is a small hill at the back of Drumnadrochit with a magnificent view of Loch Ness, and I was bewitched by its magick. Craigmonie is part of Balmacaan Woods, a forest that is creepy, overgrown, rich, green, and fecund with flying insects and has many sacred groves and paths. My friends and I became scarily lost there one fine summer's day: it was as though the trees kept repeating themselves and corralling us into one place, because no matter what we did we always ended up in the same spot in the middle of the forest. The whole adventure left me with a weird, spaced-out feeling. In retrospect, I think we were being messed with by the fae!

Tomnahurich means "hill of the faeries" in Gaelic. Tomnahurich Hill is a cemetery situated south-west of Inverness town centre, and according to legend Thomas the Rhymer, the famous 13th-century seer, is buried there. The energy there is incredible, and I walked and picnicked there to read my tarot cards and enjoy the peacefulness of nature.

One time I was in emotional turmoil about something, and had gone hoofing up the hill to seek some solitude and head space. Such was my haste that I tripped and was about to go rolling down a steep hill when I felt my whole body being pulled quickly upright by . . . something. What was it? I still don't know, but always assumed it was a kind faery whose helping hand just at the right time saved me from substantial injury.

In Australia in the Perth Hills my parents' house backs on to a bush reserve full of gum trees and other native plants. One evening my sister, our friend and me were sitting on the veranda overlooking the reserve when, suddenly, a bright light about the size of a small coin came zipping up to my face. It flitted from left to right, to left again, then scooted away as quickly as it had appeared. I was stunned.

I asked my sister and friend whether they had seen it, but they had not. I was concerned, because they were both looking as me as though I was mad. Clearly, something odd had happened, and we went inside and didn't speak about it for the rest of the night. My own practice honors faery energy, and although it might be different for you this is my experience. My favorite way to connect with the fae is to go to a beautiful, secluded place in nature and just listen. I take my tarot or oracle cards with me and ask them questions, and they speak through the cards. I like to honor the fae for the joy and delight they bring me, the quiet communion with nature, the insights, and the sense of magick.

A word to the wise: when you're working with the fae and/or asking favors do not demand or be grabby, as they can see into your heart and your true intentions and do not like being bossed around. Would you?

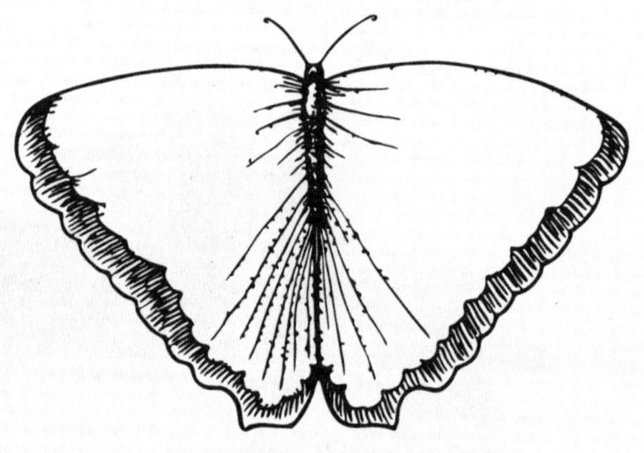

Your magickal name

When you first start working with energy on the witchcraft path you may want to give yourself a magickal name. Names carry energy, and the sound they make carries a certain resonance. Your magickal name is one that is special to you and helps you step into your power as an energy worker. When I came back from Scotland and started on the path of the kitchen witch in earnest my magickal name became Priestess Moon: "Priestess" to honor the feminine power of the goddess, and "Moon" as I chose to work very closely with the phases of the moon in my spells and rituals.

It may help you to write down the things that are important to you such as the elements, trees, animals, or celestial objects and come up with a special name through that process. Your magickal name is uniquely you and will feel just right.

How to use this book

Think of this book as a buffet of spells you can pick and choose as you need, such as love, luck, or protection. Choose your preferred spell, gather your ingredients, then set aside a quiet moment to perform your magick. Like any recipe book, each spell has an ingredients and method section.

The stickers in this book are often included as part of the spells: some are there to seal your spell with extra magick once you have performed the spell, and some are just for fun. Each recipe has its own journal page where you can write down any insights or recipe changes, thus creating your own book of shadows as you work through this grimoire.

This book uses plant magick, which involves working with the spiritual properties of plants as you craft your spells. There are 37 plants and herbs to choose from and create magick within this book. Each plant is said to have an energetic signature that can be used for a specific goal; for example, basil for luck, roses for love, rosemary for protection, and lavender to balance and heal.

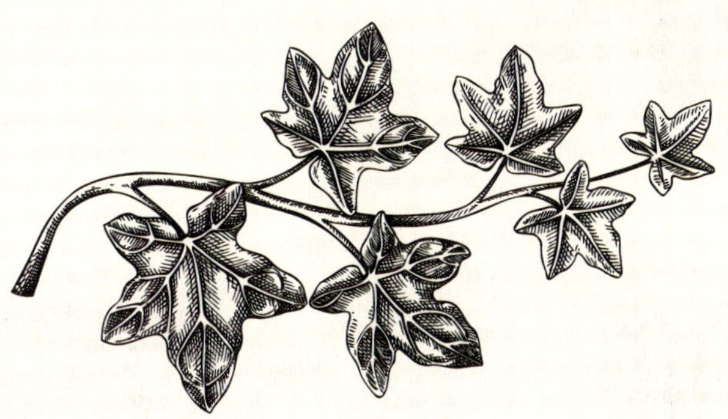

Intention is everything, so when you perform a spell fully expect to have what you have asked for. If it is for your highest good, you *shall* have it. To get started:

- Choose a spell.
- Gather the ingredients.
- Perform a ritual (see "Before starting spell work" below).
- Follow the instructions in the recipe.
- Write down any insights in the journal section and seal the spell with the corresponding plant potion sticker by placing it in the circle provided and saying: "So mote it be."
- Ground yourself by clapping your hands or eating something delicious.

Before starting spell work

The first step for any spell work is to create a magickal space. Carve out a little place for yourself such as a shelf, table, or little nook in a favorite room that is yours. It will usually display your treasured and sacred things.

Before beginning any psychic work it's important to protect your energy by consciously calling a circle of protection around you in the form of white light. As well, you could call upon Archangel Michael for protection by imagining being bathed in a beam of electric blue light from this powerful angel. The following visualization is a wonderful way to lighten the energy around you before you spell craft:

- To begin with, burn a sage smudge stick or your favourite incense.
- Take a deep breath and imagine a bubble of bright white light surrounding you. Call in your guides and angels.
- Imagine a golden light starting from above your head and moving all the way past your feet into the molten core of Mother Earth.

- Visualize this light connecting with the core, then moving up through your body and into the sky as high as you can imagine it, eventually coming to rest in your heart area and surrounding your whole body in light. Affirm that you are safe and protected.
- You can now start your spell work.
- Spells are a creative form of manifesting and goal setting. It's a good idea to write down your intent for the spell at this point, stating your desired outcome. Affirm that your spell work will be for the greater good of all.

Edible spells

Like *Alice in Wonderland*, the *Witch's Magickal Spellbook* is meant to be a delightful journey of discovery, but you should use your common sense when eating or drinking edible spells. Obviously, if you are allergic to a certain ingredient do not use it, but instead substitute it with one you can eat. Play and experiment with the recipes. Some of the recipes use edible gold leaf, which can be found at most specialty kitchen stores or online; it must be marked as edible, and you can use the same packet for multiple recipes. It is an optional ingredient but it does add a visual boost, especially to money spells.

Spells as prayers

Spells are prayers in action. You have a wish or desire and want to be able to work on this at an energetic level, an unseen level, to bring the wish about. You can get creative and make the prayer more personal and hands on by using items such as flowers, herbs, and crystals that you feel will bring a certain extra energy to the prayer. A charm, ritual, or recipe can help you focus on the positive quality you would like to bring into your life.

Helpful tools for spell work

The following are some tools to choose from to help you enhance your enchantments.

Moon magic: the phases of the moon can bring more power to your spells. As a rule, the energy of a new moon is to start projects and attract things, so this is a great time for money or luck spells. A waxing crescent to full moon is to complete things and is great for love spells. A waning to dark moon is used to let things go or get rid of things you do not want. This would be a good time to perform protection or banishing spells.

Candle and color magic: you can use color magick to add another boost to your charms, and it can be as simple as colored candles or paper. When the spell asks for candles or paper you can use neutral white every time, or you can mix it up and add color to take advantage of color magick:

- white for strong protection and shielding
- black for letting go and releasing
- red for love and vitality
- orange for fertility and creativity
- yellow for confidence and fame
- green for healing and good luck
- blue for wisdom and contemplation
- purple for intuition and angelic assistance
- pink for love and friendship
- silver for personal power and abundance
- gold for money spells.

Never leave a candle burning unattended. If you are concerned about the safety of a burning candle you could use a battery-operated one.

The spells

Spin the wheel to create a circle of protection around you before you craft.

Prosperity

Alfalfa money amulet

Ginger business-attracting charm

Grapefruit money spell

Saffron liquid-gold elixir

Tomato prosperity pomander

How prosperity spells work

Money and wealth can be tricky things: there seems to be a direct correlation between what you think you deserve and what you end up getting. Prosperity consciousness is the idea that if you allow yourself to receive more you will attract more to you. Your thought of "I deserve this!" sets up a frequency that attracts more wealth, money, and prosperity into your world. You put the thought out there with the intention to live a more prosperous life, and eventually this has no other choice but to happen as this is what you are focusing on.

When you surrender and trust that you will be always taken care of in a material sense your trust will be rewarded. The tricky part is surrendering without allowing any thoughts about that not being the way this world works, which brings in scarcity energy. Perhaps that was once true: it used to be harder to create prosperity on this earth, but it's different now. Just try it!

How much money do you think you deserve and will be comfortable with? You might be surprised that you have a limit when you think of the top amount you deserve. Is it $100,000, $1 million, $10 million? Why are you imposing that limit on yourself? This is when your belief systems about money can be holding you back. You may also find yourself judging others on the amount of money they have, and how they choose to spend it. This is another belief that uncovers how much you think you deserve and how much you think others deserve. It's worth exploring these limiting beliefs as part of your commitment toward a more abundant life. A focus on prosperity and wealth can become a daily habit, where you change those thoughts of "never enough" to "I always have enough" and see how it affects the reality of your lived experience.

Money energy is circular: the more generous you are with yourself and others the more money will be attracted to you. The more you believe you deserve the more you will attract, but I agree it's not easy in a world where the basic needs of life such as warmth, food, and shelter have high costs associated with them.

According to some spiritual teachers there are bands of energy that surround the earth. Some examples are fear and scarcity, and others are bands of joy and prosperity. It's your thoughts and frequency that will match certain bands of energy. Which frequency would you like to tap in to? Make a conscious decision to choose prosperity instead of letting thoughts of scarcity and lack keep running the same old programs through your mind. Be open to the different ways abundance can show up in your life. It may not be just money: it could be gifts and experiences as well.

Back in the early 2000s my mum, sister, and I formed a "creating money" group, inspired by the excellent book of the same name by Sanaya Roman. We met once a week and went through a chapter in the book and did the exercises at the end of each chapter. One thing that really stood out for me is that during this time my mum won $1,000 in the lottery. The very next week her car needed $1,000 worth of maintenance. Easy come, easy go, but there was great joy and amazement that consciously working with money energy in a positive way had brought fruitful results.

A certain amount of money you want to manifest may not show up in a whole amount. As an example, when I tried the grapefruit spell in this chapter I wrote down the amount of $250. Interestingly, the money did not come in a single lump sum, but within a week I had received an unexpected refund and a cash gift, and I even found some money in the glove compartment of my car. All of these amounts added up to the near total I was trying to manifest. Keep an open mind and remember that, at least initially, it is often easier to manifest smaller amounts of money when you are trying to work out how much you will allow yourself.

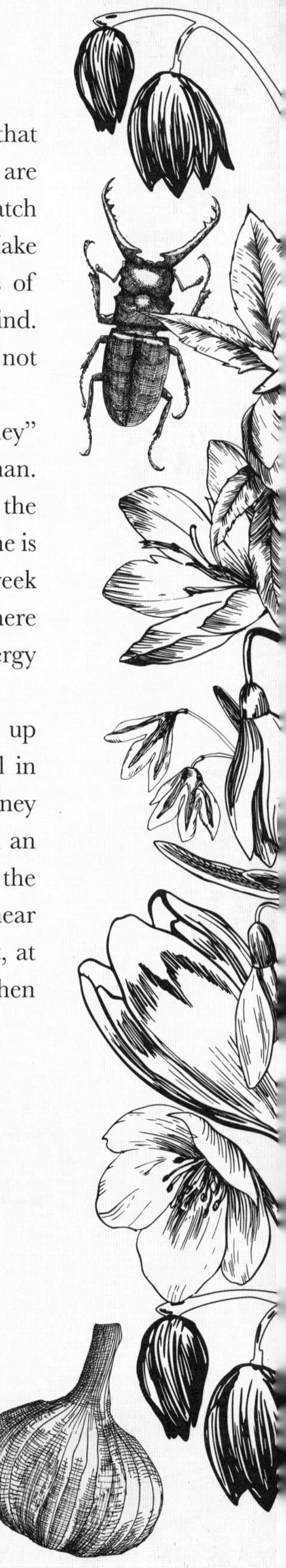

Alfalfa

I joyfully attract money.

Scientific name

Medicago sativa

Healing properties

Alfalfa, an excellent anti-oxidant, may lower blood pressure and cholesterol and acts as a diuretic.

MAGICKAL USES

Alfalfa grows well and quickly, making it the perfect herb to use in money spells. Its leaves resemble the clover leaf. Clovers are considered to be lucky in Irish folklore as their three leaves were likened to the holy trinity by St Patrick, but even before that it was noticed that wherever clover grew the soil was rich and fertile. In the context of sympathetic magick, fast-growing, hardy plants are excellent for fast money spells. Alfalfa is associated with the root chakra.

Alfalfa money amulet

This spell is for attracting money.

The lucky alfalfa juice and the gold coins on the alfalfa illustration encourage a mindset for attracting wealth.

INGREDIENTS

1 large alfalfa money amulet sticker • 3.5 in x 2 in | 9 cm x 5.5 cm piece of cardboard • 3.5 in x 2 in | 9 cm x 5.5 cm laminating pouch • laminator • 1 cup alfalfa shoots • 15.5. in x 15.5. in | 40 cm x 40 cm piece of muslin cloth

METHOD

Place the alfalfa money amulet sticker onto the cardboard and laminate to protect the sticker.

Crush the alfalfa shoots in a food processor or with a mortar and pestle. Place a wire mesh strainer over a glass bowl and strain the pulp through the muslin, lightly pressing to extract the liquid. Discard the pulp and strain the juice again through the muslin. It will yield about 2 teaspoons of liquid.

Dab the resulting clear liquid onto your money amulet and say: "I joyfully attract money!" Keep the amulet in your purse or wallet to attract wealth. You could even dab this magick liquid onto lotto cards or cash to bring an increase in wealth.

JOURNAL
Once you have performed the spell affix the alfalfa sticker in the circle, affirming: "So mote it be."

Ginger

I joyfully attract new business and money.

Scientific name

Zingiber officinale

Healing properties

Ginger helps settle your stomach and can enhance your mood by working with serotonin receptors in the brain.

MAGICKAL USES

The heat of ginger is said to amplify spells, making the achievement of the desired results come more quickly. Ginger is associated with the root chakra, which is the power centre responsible for you feeling safe and secure. On a metaphysical level, ginger brings the power to achieve results and boosts self-esteem, giving you the confidence to share your work with the world.

Ginger business-attracting charm

This spell is for attracting new customers and increasing business sales.

When you use your business card, gold coins, and the magick-attracting power of ginger you will be sending out a positive frequency to attract more clients and sales.

INGREDIENTS

1 gold candle • your business card • 2 in | 5 cm piece of ginger sliced into three round discs • 3 gold coins

METHOD

Light the gold candle. Place the business card in front of the candle and the three discs of ginger around the card.

As you place each gold coin on top of a piece of ginger, say: "I joyfully attract new business and money!"

Leave the candle to safely burn and imagine the money and ginger acting as a golden magnet for customers to find you, bringing new business and wealth.

JOURNAL

Once you have performed the spell affix the grapefruit potion sticker in the circle, affirming: "So mote it be."

Grapefruit

I am a magnet for money miracles.

Scientific name

Citrus × paradisi

Healing properties

Grapefruit refreshes and stimulates your liver and has an uplifting effect on mood. Rub the essential oil on your temples to help relieve a migraine.

MAGICKAL USES

The grapefruit has long been associated with prosperity and generosity, making it perfect for money spells. Grapefruits are associated with the third eye chakra and are excellent for bringing clarity to a situation. When you are making important decisions to do with finances, burn some grapefruit essential oil and ask to be given a clear picture of the best choice for you in this moment.

Grapefruit money spell

This spell is for manifesting a certain amount of money.

See how long it takes for this spell to manifest the amount of money you're aiming for: it may surprise you!

INGREDIENTS

a pen • 1 piece of yellow paper • 3 drops of grapefruit essential oil or juice from a grapefruit • grapefruit potion sticker

METHOD

Work out the exact amount of money you need: it may be for a holiday, new car, to pay a bill, or some savi eel safe. Write the amount, which needs to feel real to you and on the paper with the pen.

Wr s.

Pou te:

JOURNAL

Once you have performed the spell affix the grapefruit potion sticker in the circle, affirming: "So mote it be."

Saffron

I increase my wealth and blessings by focusing on all the good in my life.

Scientific name

Crocus sativus

Healing properties

With its anti-inflammatory properties, saffron can help improve digestion and brain function. A tincture may help lung conditions.

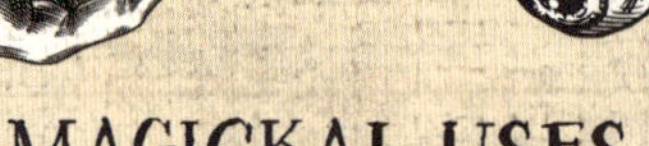

MAGICKAL USES

Saffron is exceedingly rare and therefore expensive, so it has become a symbol of wealth and prosperity. The use of saffron in meals is said to attract abundance to you and your guests by adding a sense of luxury to the feast. In some cultures, saffron offers a protective quality and is used in the form of smoke to dispel unwanted energies. It is associated with the gorgeous orange color of the sacral chakra.

Saffron liquid-gold elixir

This spell is for attracting wealth.

By ingesting the beautiful golden liquid of warm saffron, you are inviting wealth into your life.

INGREDIENTS

3 strands of saffron • 1 small teacup • freshly boiled water • honey, to taste • edible gold leaf, optional

METHOD

Place the saffron threads into the teacup, pour in the boiled water and stir in the honey if using. Top with edible gold leaf for a truly prosperous potion.

As you sip the liquid-gold elixir remember all the things you already have in your life that make you feel prosperous and write them on the journal page. It may be a warm bed, enough to eat, dear loved ones, or joyful activities.

While sipping the elixir affirm: "I increase my wealth and blessings by focusing on all the good in my life."

JOURNAL
Once you have performed the spell affix the saffron potion sticker in the circle, affirming: "So mote it be."

Tomato

I think, speak, and act as though I am already wealthy

Scientific name

Solanum lycopersicum

Healing properties

Tomatoes leaves can be made into a poultice to heal your skin. Anecdotally, a slice of tomato will clear a skin infection when regularly applied.

MAGICKAL USES

The shiny red color of a plump tomato is said to attract wealth and prosperity. Tomatoes are associated with the root chakra and are also used for love spells: they are sometimes known as "love apples," with a belief that they had aphrodisiac properties. In medieval France a bowl of tomato soup was served by young ladies to potential husbands. In this spell, however, the tomato is used to bring in positive wealth energy by imagining that your relationship with money is a wonderful one!

Tomato prosperity pomander

This spell is for attracting prosperity.

How would you act if you were already wealthy? How would you spend your time, and what would you wear? How would you treat yourself and others? Record your answers on the tomato journal page. Think about how you can incorporate these goals into your life right now so you think, speak, and act as though you are already wealthy.

INGREDIENTS

1 ripe red tomato • 2 red-topped pins • 40 in | 1 m piece red ribbon

METHOD

Secure the ribbon at the top of the tomato with a pin so there are equal lengths hanging down.

Tie one half of the ribbon as though you are tying up a gift box, securing it at the bottom of the tomato with the second pin. Tie the remaining ribbon at the top of the tomato, leaving a length of ribbon free to tie the pomander to a tree.

Hang the tomato outside your home to attract more riches to you.

JOURNAL

Once you have performed the spell affix the tomato potion sticker in the circle, affirming: "So mote it be."

I G
I G
I G

Love

Calendula self-love spell

Caraway loyal-lover mojo

Cranberry lovetini potion

Rosemary ice block shadowbox

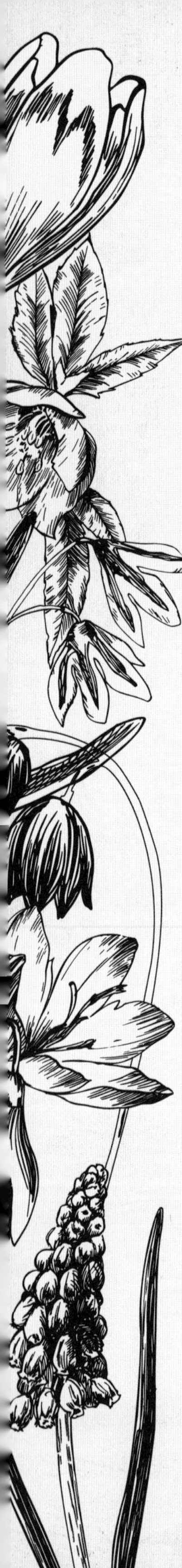

How love spells work

As a teen and young adult I experimented extensively with love spells with mixed results. Looking back, I have been extremely grateful that some of my love spells were not successful, even though I was disappointed at the time! There are spells for fun and flirtations, and then there are spells for true love and soul mates. I cannot stress enough how important it is to not focus on your latest crush when you perform a love spell. I'll admit I was naughty and did focus on my latest crush but, thankfully, these ones didn't work.

My old book of shadows from 1997, when I was in my early 20s, contained plenty of love spells, all with varying results. The most effective love spell from this time is in the guidebook for my *Enchanted Unicorn Oracle* and is called "Love Spell."

As a special treat, I am sharing here two extra love spells from my book of shadows. I warmly invite you to try them and experience their magick! The red love spell is perfect if you are looking for a little more fun and flirtation in your life; nothing serious. The cups of love spell is for a more permanent and serious relationship, helping you visualize and attract a compatible and stable partner. Both are good spells for those seeking greater connection with others.

Red love spell

My best friend and I decided to experiment with a love spell to see if we could each attract a boyfriend.

INGREDIENTS

piece of red paper • 2 red roses (we didn't have red roses so we used apricot roses from the garden) • 2 sprigs of rose geranium (the flowers were red)

METHOD

Winter, waxing moon in Capricorn, the altar set with the four elements represented: salt for earth, athame for air, chalice for water, and a candle for fire. Circle cast and the quarters called in. We wrote down specifically what we wanted in a boyfriend on a piece of red paper; it was probably "single", "wealthy," and "nice looking."

We held hands over the altar and invited in the goddess of the moon, and we were quiet and still. Suddenly, we were dancing around in a circle clockwise, chanting: "Bring love to us, and may it harm none. Bring love to us, and may it harm none" over and over again.

We wrapped one rose and one rose geranium sprig in each piece of paper, then there came a crash of lightning that illuminated the altar. We held the paper and said three times: "Goddess, may this spell come true by the next full moon." We thanked the elements and closed the circle by saying: "The circle is open but never broken."

We placed the red love spells on the altar and ate chocolate to ground the energy.

Cups of love spell

Here is another love spell I experimented with, inspired by the book *Lady of the Night* by Edain McCoy.

INGREDIENTS

3 cups • 1 seashell • 1 handmade beeswax candle, scented with the oil • rose geranium essential oil

METHOD

Summer, waning crescent moon in Capricorn: the circle is cast and the quarters called in. Half-fill two of the cups with water and place them at opposite sides of your altar. Place the third cup, empty, in the middle. Scent the candle with the essential oil, light it and say a prayer to the goddess.

Focus on the empty middle cup and visualize that the relationship you want is coming alive within it. Bring the other two cups, one representing you and one representing your true love, together and pour the water from each one into the empty cup. Watch the water mingle and become one. Add a single drop of the essential oil. Place the shell in this cup and see the water glowing with the red light of passion: the shell will be anointed with the oil and your intention. Wear the shell every day as a talisman until the moon phase changes.

The truth is these love spells had mixed results. In hindsight, I was not ready for a serious relationship and really had to get to know myself better first. You can do as many love spells as you like and they can result in fun and flirtations, and that's fine if that's all you want. However, if you are truly ready for a serious relationship it will find you at just the right time, love spell or not. You have to be open to who is best for you, not who you think you should be with. I promise you that if someone was meant for you, you will be with them.

What's more, this person could end up being a delicious surprise! Focus on the qualities you want in a person, how they make you feel, compatibility, and emotional resonance. Looks and financial stability could also be part of this if that is important to you, but it's best if this is not the main focus. I think the old adage is true: you need to learn to love yourself first, which is why I have included love spells for the self in this section.

JOURNAL
Did you try the red love and
cups of love spells? Write
down what happened.

Calendula

I focus on the beauty within myself.

Scientific name

Calendula officinalis

Healing properties

Calendula oil makes an excellent skin tonic. When applied to your face it will create a healthy glow and regenerate the skin.

MAGICKAL USES

Calendula is a bright, sunny, yellow flower and is often used in love spells to bring happiness. It is associated with the golden color of the solar plexus chakra and, as such, can inspire feelings of confidence and worthiness. It can burn away the energy of old wounds and thoughts that no longer serve you and bring in a very positive healing experience. Work with calendula to boost your self-esteem.

Calendula self-love spell

This spell is for discovering your unique talents and gifts.

Write down 10 things you love about yourself in the frames provided. Seal each frame with a calendula flower sticker.

JOURNAL

Once you have performed the spell affix the calendula potion sticker in the circle, affirming: "So mote it be."

Caraway

I am ready to commit to a faithful relationship.

Scientific name

Carum carvi

Healing properties

Caraway seeds freshen your breath and aid digestion, and are often used as a cure for colic. Powdered, use in a poultice to help heal bruises.

MAGICKAL USES

Caraway is a protective herb, especially in matters of love, and is said to help keep your partner loyal. The warmth of caraway is associated with the solar plexus chakra and can help bring confidence in relationships. It is also a protective herb, often used in spells to protect from mischievous energies. Add caraway to wedding bouquets to ensure a long and faithful marriage.

Caraway loyal-lover mojo

This spell is for keeping a lover loyal.

Love spells are at their most pure when the focus is on the self, not the other person.

INGREDIENTS

1 small rose quartz crystal • 2 tablespoons dried caraway seeds • 2 tablespoons dried rose petals • 1 red or pink drawstring bag • 2 drops of rose or rose geranium essential oil

METHOD

Place the crystal, caraway seeds and rose petals in the bag. There will be an aroma of roses and warm, sweet caraway. Add the rose oil for extra sweetness.

Affirm to yourself that you are now ready to commit to an authentic relationship, where you and your partner are loyal and faithful to each other. Keep the mojo under your pillow and allow yourself to trust that your love will be true.

JOURNAL
Once you have performed the spell affix the caraway potion sticker in the circle, affirming: "So mote it be."

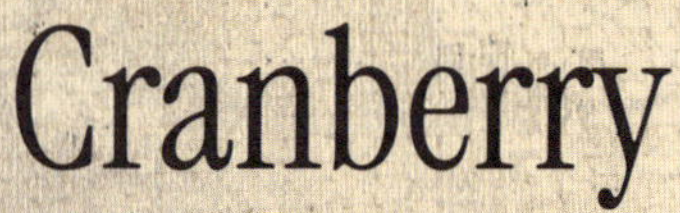

Cranberry

I attract joyful connections and flirtations.

Scientific name

Vaccinium ocicocos

Healing properties

Astringent cranberry juice makes an excellent healing tonic for your kidneys and bladder.

MAGICKAL USES

Cranberries are used in love spells because of their passionate red color, and are associated with the root chakra. Cranberry juice is often used in iconic cocktails and mocktails, adding to the fun and flirty energy of this plant. Love potions are a strong theme in myth and magick, where a special elixir is consumed by an unsuspecting paramour. In this case, you are in full control and are drinking the love potion yourself.

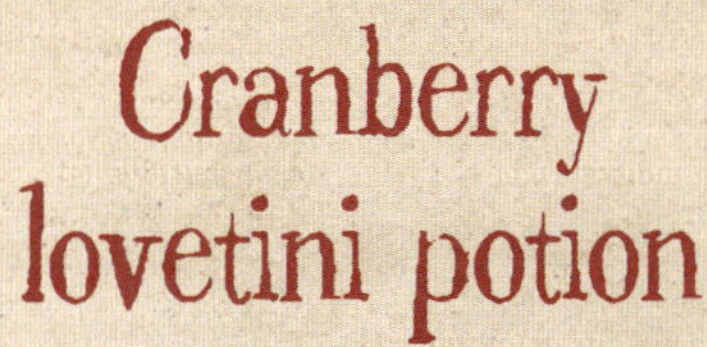

Cranberry lovetini potion

This spell is for attracting joyful and playful connections with others.

A delicious mocktail before attending a party is always a fabulous idea!

INGREDIENTS

1⅔ fl oz | 50 ml cranberry juice • 1⅔ fl oz | 50 ml fresh mandarin or orange juice • ⅓ fl oz | 10 ml fresh lime juice • 1 teaspoon maple syrup • dash of vanilla essence • ice • cocktail shaker • martini glass • 1 strawberry

METHOD

Place the liquid ingredients over the ice in the cocktail shaker and shake, shall we say about 10 times? Pour into the chilled martini glass and garnish with the strawberry.

As you drink your love potion imagine you are attracting the perfect partner to play with.

JOURNAL
Once you have performed the spell affix the cranberry potion sticker in the circle, affirming: "So mote it be."

Rosemary

I say goodbye to the past and look forward to the future.

Scientific name

Salvia rosmarinus

Healing properties

Sharp and herbaceous rosemary can help improve your memory and is an excellent tonic for lung and liver conditions.

MAGICKAL USES

Rosemary is perfect for protection and purification spells to ward off negative energies. It is said that if a rosemary bush is growing at the front of the house the nurturing and protective feminine energy is in charge. Rosemary can also combat sickness with its resinous scent and shielding frequency. It is associated with the heart chakra and can strengthen self-love by showing you what you will and will not accept from others.

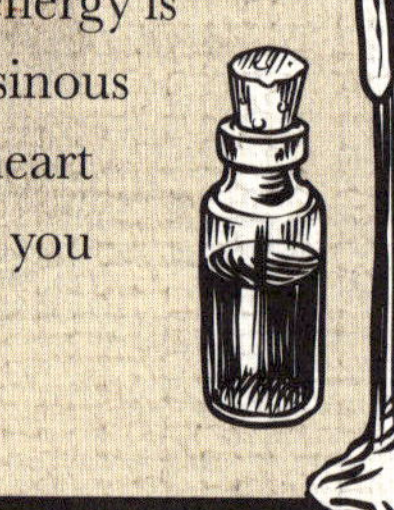

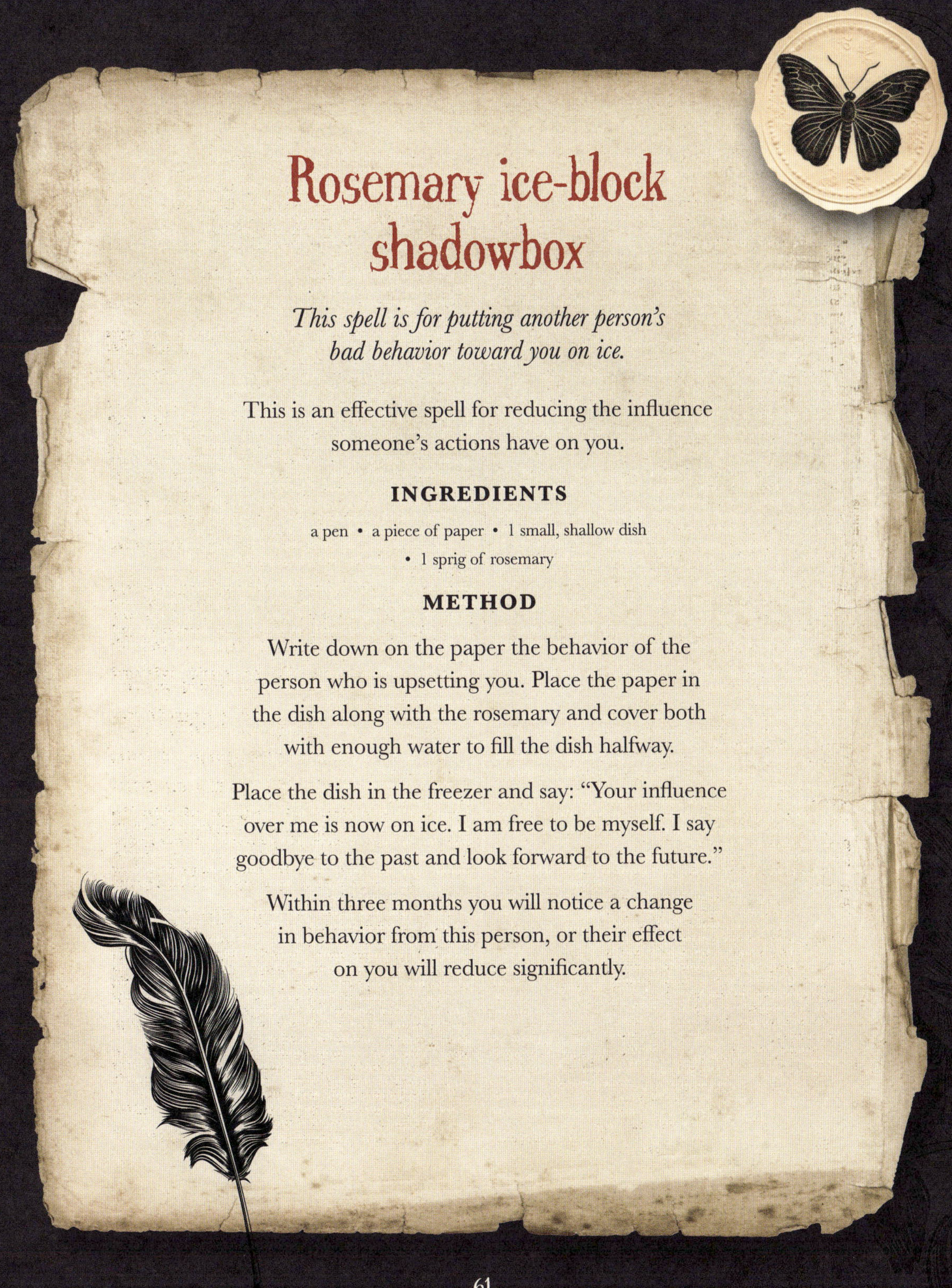

Rosemary ice-block shadowbox

This spell is for putting another person's bad behavior toward you on ice.

This is an effective spell for reducing the influence someone's actions have on you.

INGREDIENTS

a pen • a piece of paper • 1 small, shallow dish • 1 sprig of rosemary

METHOD

Write down on the paper the behavior of the person who is upsetting you. Place the paper in the dish along with the rosemary and cover both with enough water to fill the dish halfway.

Place the dish in the freezer and say: "Your influence over me is now on ice. I am free to be myself. I say goodbye to the past and look forward to the future."

Within three months you will notice a change in behavior from this person, or their effect on you will reduce significantly.

JOURNAL

Once you have performed the spell affix the rosemary potion sticker in the circle, affirming: "So mote it be."

A
AB
ABR
ABRA
ABRAC
ABRACA
ABRACAD
ABRACADA
ABRACADAB
ABRACADABR
ABRACADABRA

Luck

Basil luck spell

Elderflower home blessing

Nasturtium fairy luck talisman

Vanilla three wishes charm

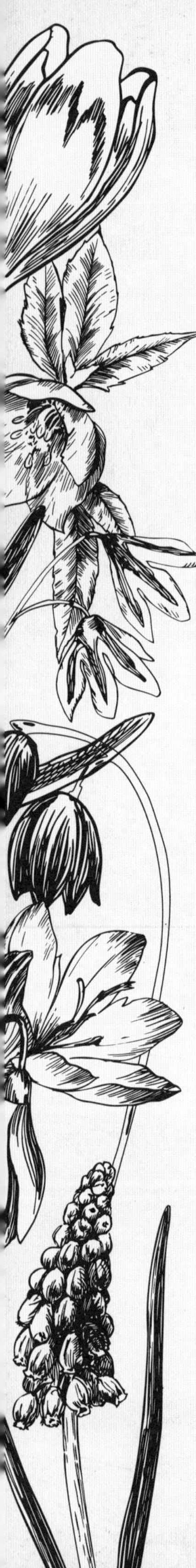

How luck spells work

You will attract luck when you have a light heart and are open to possibilities. Luck means not being tied to a certain outcome such as winning the lottery but, instead, being receptive to receiving lucky gifts and surprises from many sources. Learn how to say "Yes" to unexpected opportunities. In my experience, working with the faery folk can bring in delightful good fortune, especially when you are honest and your intentions are pure. I've added some of my experiences with the faery folk in the "Working with the fae" section on page 4 to give you an idea of how this kind of luck can show up in your life.

I have found you attract luck when you are being your most authentic self, which means speaking your truth and not masking your true feelings or trying to people please all the time. When your true self shines through lucky events and opportunities start to match your frequency.

When I was living in Scotland I was in a very expanded state, saying "Yes" to a lot of opportunities, and traveling wherever the wind and my intuition took me. I ended up settling in a little village called Lewiston on the banks of the River Ness for a wee while. At the back of the town was a small mountain called Craigmonie, a place full of magick that has a beautiful view of Loch Ness that I regularly visited. My friend and I went up there to do some spell work and I remember writing wishes on a rock I found and drawing some of the trees I could see. The place is alive with faery energy; I could feel them! We shouted our wishes into the trees and rocks, and the wind started whipping around us. The skies opened and suddenly a storm was upon us. We quickly scurried back down the hill to find shelter.

I was living and working in a small 19th-century hotel in the village at the time that was said to be (and actually was) haunted, but that is a story for another time. The morning after the storm I woke up and saw a shiny golden pound coin next to my bed. "Score!" I thought. There was another shiny gold coin just near the door to my room that I picked up, and I found two more golden coins on the stairs. I was delighted and surprised. I started the preparations for lunch service and found another coin on the restaurant floor. I was actually getting a little freaked out by now, but I was still pocketing the money! A few more coins appeared around the hotel, until I found the last coin outside near the picnic tables. I ended up with around £11 in gold coins that day, and I link this lucky find directly to the little spell rock I had created on the magickal hill. I just couldn't find any other explanation for the appearance of so many coins being dotted around the hotel. I treated myself and my friend to a few drinks that night.

This kind of magic is called an "apport," which is when an object or objects seemingly materialize out of thin air from the spirit realm. As a fun little game, ask your guides to apport a shiny golden coin for you in the next week and see what happens!

The spells in this section bring in faery energy to attract luck into your realm. The nasturtium faery luck talisman on page 77 is inspired by a 4,500 BCE stone carving called the Great Glyph, discovered in a stone chamber by archeologists in Ireland. According to legend, this symbol has been gifted to the human race by the Sidhe, the faery race of ancient Ireland, to help humans connect with them as spiritual seekers.

Basil

I am a magnet for good luck.

Scientific name

Ocimum basilicum

Healing properties

Basil heals and soothes your digestive system, and the crushed leaves can be used to treat insect bites. The essential oil can help with a headache.

MAGICKAL USES

The lucky bright green color of basil, plus its fast-growing nature, make it perfect for luck spells. Basil is associated with the third eye chakra and can activate an elevated consciousness and clarity in the spiritual seeker. In certain Christian Orthodox traditions it is seen as a herb for purification and protection. It is placed around church altars and within holy water to ward of negative entities and, funnily enough, witches.

Basil luck spell

This spell is for attracting fortunate events and lucky surprises.

When you visualize the emerald-green color of basil throughout your aura you will start to magnetize lucky events and synchronicities.

INGREDIENTS

foot bath or container that fits your feet • warm water • ¼ cup sea salt • 3 sprigs of basil

METHOD

Fill the foot bath with the warm water and salt.

Pluck and crush the basil leaves between your fingers, inhaling the herbaceous aroma, and place the leaves into the bath. Imagine that each time you do this you are filling the bath with luck.

Soak your feet in the bath, feeling the lucky green energy of the fae rising from your feet to the top of your head as though you are becoming a beacon for luck.

As you bathe your feet affirm to yourself:
"I am a magnet for good luck."

JOURNAL
Once you have performed the spell affix the basil potion sticker in the circle, affirming: "So mote it be."

Elderflower

May the faery folk bless my home with love, luck and magick.

Scientific name

Sambuccus spp.

Healing properties

Elderflower is an anti-inflammatory plant; its flowers are used in tinctures to help improve your immune system.

MAGICKAL USES

Associated with the faery folk, the elderflower tree is often used in spells for house blessings and protection. The elder tree is sacred in the Druid tradition, in which it is referred to as the tree of life. Elder magic is one of speaking your truth, especially speaking out against people and corporations that are harming the environment. Thus it is connected with the throat chakra.

Elderflower home blessing

This spell is for blessing a new home or to add blessings and luck to an existing one.

This spell is best performed at the start of the new year, or at a new moon to bring fresh energy into your living space.

INGREDIENTS

2 twigs from an elderflower tree about 8 in | 20 cm in length each
• 1 cup fresh water • 6.5 ft | 2 m length of green ribbon

METHOD

Before taking the twigs from the elder tree ask for the tree's permission, and pour the water at the base as a gift to the tree.

Lay the two cut twigs in an equal cross shape. Bind them together with the green ribbon, winding it up and back down each of the four lengths of the cross and tying the end of the ribbon to one of the sticks.

As you work say: "To the north, to the east, to the south, and to the west, may the faery folk bless my home with love, luck, and magick."

Display the elderflower house blessing in your kitchen or on your altar to ensure your house is filled with luck and blessings for the months or year ahead.

JOURNAL

Once you have performed the spell affix the elderflower potion sticker in the circle, affirming: "So mote it be."

Nasturtium

The luck of the fae is with me today.

Scientific name

Tropaeolum majus

Healing properties

Crushed nasturtium leaves can be used as a poultice for troublesome skin conditions. The flowers are also edible and make a lovely addition to salads .

MAGICKAL USES

Nasturtium leaves resemble shields, making them suitable in protection spells. They also physically protect plants from aphids and beetles. The sunny yellow-orange flowers are said to bring luck and happiness. Nasturtium is connected with the vitality of the sacral chakra, bringing balance and healing to the emotional body. They are associated with the faery folk, especially those who love to play around wildflowers.

Nasturtium faery luck talisman

This spell is for attracting the luck of the fae.

The symbol in this luck talisman is a gift from the Sidhe in Ireland, an ancient race of faery beings.

INGREDIENTS

1 circular faery luck talisman sticker • 2 in x 2 in | 5.5 cm x 5.5 cm piece of gold cardboard • 3.5 in x 2 in | 9 cm x 5.5 cm laminating pouch • laminator

METHOD

Place the sticker on the cardboard and laminate to protect the sticker. Cut to size.

Display the talisman in a prominent place, and each time you see it ask the faeries to bless you with good luck by saying: "The luck of the fae is with me today!"

For an extra-lucky day, you can also carry the symbol with you when you go out.

JOURNAL

Once you have performed the spell affix the nasturtium potion sticker in the circle, affirming: "So mote it be."

Vanilla

I make three wishes, and it would be wonderful if they came true.

Scientific name

Vanilla planifolia

Healing properties

Eating or smelling pure vanilla can help calm your nervous system. It's used in face creams for its anti-aging properties.

MAGICKAL USES

Although used in love spells, more often vanilla is used in luck or money spells because the expensive vanilla bean is considered to be a luxury. It is connected with the sensuality of the sacral chakra and is oft used in perfumes to bewitch and beguile. As a simple love spell, bake a vanilla cake and ice with vanilla buttercream icing. As you add strawberries on top, state out loud each quality you would like in a potential partner.

Vanilla three wishes charm

This spell is for asking for three wishes to come true.

Focusing on the things that you want helps bring that energy into your consciousness: you will start to believe in the possibilities! This spell is inspired by the three wishes the genie grants Aladdin when he cleans the magic lamp.

INGREDIENTS

a pen • 3 pieces of paper • 3 drops of vanilla essence or extract • vanilla potion bottle sticker

METHOD

Write down a wish on each piece of paper: you get three wishes.

Dab a drop of vanilla essence on each wish and place them in the envelope below. Seal the envelope with the vanilla potion bottle sticker and say: "I make three wishes, and it would be wonderful if they came true."

Come back to this envelope in a year's time to see which of the wishes have come true.

JOURNAL

Once you have performed the spell affix the vanilla potion sticker in the circle, affirming: "So mote it be."

Healing
Arnica meditation mandala
Blueberry magick ice
Celery anti-commotion potion
Ginseng energy charm
Magick plum pill

How healing spells work

Many spiritual texts state that dis-ease begins in the aura, the energetic template that surrounds your physical body. This is first manifested by your thought patterns and interactions with others. Consider this theory: every time you damp down your words and behaviors to make everyone around you comfortable apart from yourself, the chinks begin to appear in your energy body.

You may have a friend or family member that, for whatever reason, thinks it is funny to jokingly put you down, and when you have said something in the past about it they have called you too sensitive or said you can't take a joke. You thus learned to be quiet and not say anything. This person continually crossed the boundary but you didn't say anything, so the chink in your energy template grew wider and wider until a certain ailment became manifest in your physical body, most likely in the throat and neck area as you had been swallowing your words for so long.

Generally speaking, the part of your body the disease manifests in can give you a clue about the feelings and circumstances that may have caused it. This is nowhere near a comprehensive list, but it is a start:

- Crown chakra, head: overthinking, anxiety, and a loss of connection with the spiritual realm, thinking this human life is the only reality. Always busy with no downtime.
- Third eye chakra, eyes: indecision and not trusting your own wisdom. Making others an authority over your life, confusion.
- Throat chakra, neck and shoulders: swallowing your words, not speaking up when you feel you have been unfairly treated, always talking to fill in the silence or not talking at all because of self-judgment or fear of judgment from others.
- Heart chakra, chest, arms, and hands: grief, feelings of loneliness and disconnection, not trusting others, unresolved heartbreak, jealousy.

- Solar plexus chakra, stomach and liver: a sense of personal power has been compromised, feeling less than, feeling as though you are a loser or victim of circumstance, disappointment, guilt.
- Sacral chakra, kidneys and reproductive area: fear, anger, resentment, fears around sex and intimacy, shame, blocking the flow of creativity and pleasure, annoyance at or dislike of a partner.
- Base chakra, bowels, legs, knees, and feet: feelings of fear about personal safety or illness, worries about money and whether you'll ever have enough to survive. Worry about change and moving forward in life.

I have learned the hard way that even though I am an empath, I need to be very aware that other people's feelings are not my responsibility.

I worked in customer service in a highly emotional industry, and no matter how unhinged someone was acting you could never say anything to them or you would lose your job. I discovered I was internalizing the customer's anger and feeling responsible, even though I had no control over the circumstances.

With a fair amount of kundalini yoga working on that specific area and journaling my feelings, plus some good old-fashioned therapy, I began to set stronger boundaries with customers and not feel so accountable for other people's emotions.

These healing spells are *not* a matter of life and death: they are charms to help you focus on the health of your mind, body, and spirit, and to maintain a clear energy body. Healing begins with self-healing and self-care, allowing time to rest, dream, and potter around. These work because you are creating a space to let healing flow in without being so busy, busy, busy! Enjoy the following moments of peace, positive words, gratitude, strong emotional boundaries, and a delicious, reviving snack.

Arnica

My mind and body feel restored.

Scientific name

Arnica montana

Healing properties

Arnica flowers are used in creams and tinctures to quicken the healing of sprains and bruises. Use as a treatment for hair growth.

MAGICKAL USES

Arnica is used in healing spells because of its beautiful restorative nature. Connected with the solar plexus chakra, it inspires strength and resilience in situations where your energy is being drained by people or situations. Before you head into a place or meet with a person you know you will have trouble with, fill a small bag with dried arnica flowers to carry with you.

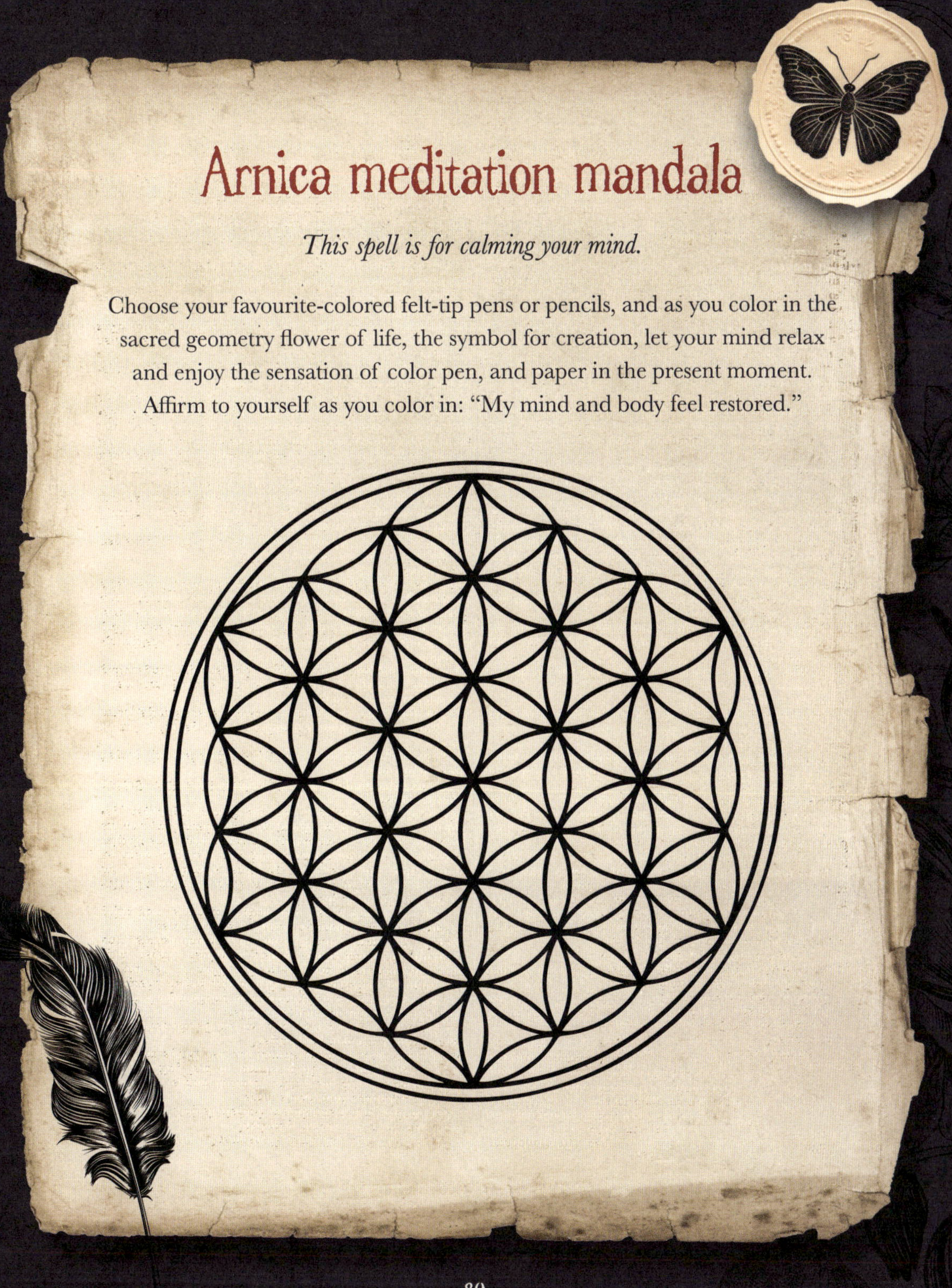

Arnica meditation mandala

This spell is for calming your mind.

Choose your favourite-colored felt-tip pens or pencils, and as you color in the sacred geometry flower of life, the symbol for creation, let your mind relax and enjoy the sensation of color pen, and paper in the present moment. Affirm to yourself as you color in: "My mind and body feel restored."

JOURNAL

Once you have performed the spell affix the arnica potion sticker in the circle, affirming: "So mote it be."

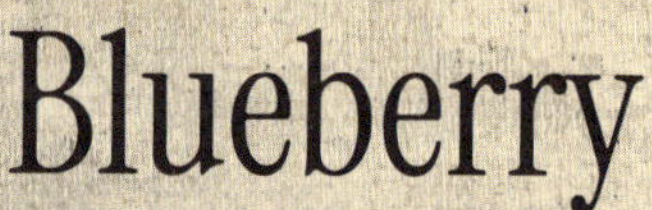

Blueberry

My cells are healthy, happy, and filled with light.

Scientific name

Vaccinium sect. *Cyanococcus*

Healing properties

Blueberries are high in anti-oxidants, and act as a great anti-inflammatory that brings healing to your skin and digestive system.

MAGICKAL USES

Blueberries can be used in a variety of magickal ways from love to protection spells, but because of their reputation as a superfood they are excellent for healing spells. The gorgeous dark-purple color of blueberries is connected with the third eye chakra and psychic abilities. With heightened perception and an ability to see clearly, you can direct healing energy to yourself and others.

Blueberry magick ice

This spell is for boosting your immune system.

This is a simple spell but one that focuses your mind on the cells in your body, which absolutely do respond to positive words.

INGREDIENTS

36 blueberries • 12-block ice tray

METHOD

Place 3 blueberries in each of the ice tray squares and fill them with water. If you want clear ice then boil and cool the water first. Freeze until the water is solid.

As you enjoy your blueberry ice blocks in your favourite beverage say to yourself: "My cells are healthy, happy, and filled with light." Imagine your cells filling with light, thanking them for all the wonderful ways they keep your body functioning.

JOURNAL
Once you have performed the spell affix the blueberry potion sticker in the circle, affirming: "So mote it be."

Celery

I calm my chattering mind with three deep breaths.

Scientific name

Apium graveolens

Healing properties

Celery can help lower your blood pressure and reduce excess water in your body. Alkaline, it can help reduce the effects of acidic foods.

MAGICKAL USES

Celery can be used in spells to improve your concentration and psychic powers. A simple celery protection spell involves sprinkling celery seeds at the four cardinal directions outside your home: north, east, south, and west. Celery is connected with the heart chakra, mainly because the plant is physically very good for heart health. According to folklore, witches would chew celery seeds to stop them from falling off their brooms!

Celery anti-commotion potion

This spell is for focusing your mind on the positive.

Think of this jar as your anti-commotion potion to add to when life gets overwhelming. Take three deep breaths before you write and affirm: "I am safe."

INGREDIENTS

a celery potion sticker • a jar with a lid • decorative items such as ribbons, sequins, gems, and glue • 1 teaspoon celery salt • 3 pieces of paper • a pen

METHOD

Affix the smaller celery sticker to the jar and decorate how you wish with ribbons, sequins, gems: anything!

Add the fragrant celery salt to the jar.

Write down on the pieces of paper one thing you are grateful for, one thing that brought you joy this week, and one thing you are looking forward to. Place the pieces of paper in the jar, and whenever you need a boost add three more. Keep coming back to one thing you are grateful for, one thing that brought you joy this week and one thing you are looking forward to.

JOURNAL
Once you have performed the spell affix the celery potion sticker in the circle, affirming: "So mote it be."

Ginseng

My energy is precious,
so I use it wisely.

Scientific name

Panax ginseng

Healing properties

Ginseng can improve your stamina and helps support your immune system. It can also assist in reducing fatigue.

MAGICKAL USES

Ginseng is known to bring more energy and vitality to spell work. The herb can bring balance to the nervous and immune systems and is considered to be an aphrodisiac, because it can encourage virility and thus is connected with the sacral chakra. Ginseng can be used in love spells for this reason, especially when you need to bring more passion to a relationship.

Ginseng energy charm

This spell is for preserving your precious energy.

Access to your energy should require a golden ticket: it is a rare and precious thing! Create this ginseng energy charm as a reminder to spend your energy wisely, to limit feeling scattered and overwhelmed and thus leading to burnout.

INGREDIENTS

¾ oz | 20 g dried ginseng root • 6⅔ fl oz | 200 ml small glass jar with a lid • 4⅔ fl oz | 140 ml vegetable oil • 19½ in | 50 cm length red ribbon • 1 golden ticket sticker

METHOD

Place the ginseng inside the jar, cover with the oil to preserve the energy stored in the ginseng, and tightly screw the lid on.

Tie the ribbon around the top of the jar to bring some vitality to your spell. Affix the golden ticket sticker to the jar and affirm: "My energy is precious, so I use it wisely."

Keep the jar in a prominent place as a reminder to keep most of your energy for things that bring you joy. Only say "Yes" to activities that bring you a feeling of happiness and light you up, or pause before you say "Yes" to something you are unsure about.

JOURNAL

Once you have performed the spell affix the ginseng potion sticker in the circle, affirming: "So mote it be."

Plum

Self-approval is a sweet and healing tonic.

Scientific name

Prunus domestica

Healing properties

Plum can reduce inflammation, calm anxiety, and assist in detoxifying your body. The juice may aid digestion.

MAGICKAL USES

Plums can be used in spells for renewal and overcoming obstacles. The beautiful violet color of plum is linked with the crown chakra. Wands used for healing are often made from plum wood and can connect you with your guides as you perform magick. They are associated with longevity and the ability to endure, despite harsh conditions. Plums can be used in spells to foster patience and wisdom.

Magick plum pill

This spell is for creating an instant pick-me up.

This recipe is inspired by Miracle Max's miracle pill in the movie *The Princess Bride*. While this delicious plum pill will not have exactly the same effect as it does on Westley in the movie, it *is* packed with powerful plant medicine.

INGREDIENTS

1¾ oz | 50 g pitted dried plums (prunes) • 1¾ oz | 50 g cashews • 1 tsp cocoa powder • 1 tsp sugar • few drops of macadamia nut oil • 1¾ oz | 50 g of 70 percent cocoa chocolate

METHOD

Process the plums, cashews, cocoa powder, sugar, and oil in a food processor until it forms a stiff, workable mix, a bit like play dough. Fashion into two large pill shapes, place on a tray lined with baking paper and freeze for 10 minutes.

A chocolate coating will help the pills go down more smoothly. Melt the chocolate until it is nice and smooth, about three 20-second bursts in the microwave, checking after each burst. Coat the chilled pills in the warm chocolate on both sides, and if you fancy you can top them with edible gold leaf.

Allow the pills to set. Obviously, you cannot swallow this pill all in one go, like Westley does in the movie, but the recipe does make a delicious and reviving snack you can eat in delicious bites!

JOURNAL

Once you have performed the spell affix the plum potion sticker in the circle, affirming: "So mote it be."

Protection
Angostura repelling shot
Clove purify your home mist
Licorice boundaries spell
Sage shielding spell

How protection spells work

When you want to perform a spell for protection it is usually because someone has hurt or annoyed you or crossed a sacred boundary. It can be very tempting to put a spell on that person, but the golden rule of any practice, not just witchcraft, is to never intentionally harm others. This is why curses are an absolute no-no, although oh so tempting when someone has really upset you. The spells in this section concentrate on your own energy hygiene and are for releasing, banishing, protecting, shielding, and creating good boundaries.

Protection spells are all about creating good energetic boundaries. Those with a beautiful open heart can often be taken advantage of and, more than others, need to be mindful of protecting their energy. You will know you are one of these people if you feel quite drained and tired after work and/or social interactions. A quick visualization of a white bubble of light surrounding you before you enter into any situation can be enough, but in some cases you will need stronger spells. These work because you intentionally set up an energetic boundary where you only let through what is good for you, and you release any energy that is not yours.

Traditional witchcraft invites us to call in the quarters before performing a spell as a form of protection, effectively creating a circle of good energy in which to perform your craft. The quarters are the four elements of earth, air, fire, and water, and they correspond with the cardinal points of north, east, south, and west respectively. This is known as "casting a circle." After the spell is performed, the elements are sent away to close the circle and ground the energy. A protection spell is a good place to try casting as circle, as it will give you an extra feeling of safety. As discussed in the "Working with the fae" section (see page 4), these elements contain the spirit of earth, air, fire, and water so you can work with a balance of energies. This means you can call in a sacred space wherever you are without the need for an altar or a physical structure such as a building.

Witchcraft as we know it today emerged in the northern hemisphere, and the elements for each cardinal direction are based on the geography and seasons of this hemisphere:

- north is earth, cold, winter, ice, and stillness
- east is air, spring, new life, blossoming, and awakening
- south is fire, summer, passion, completion, and action
- west is water, autumn, reflection, emotions, aging, and wisdom.

I live in Australia, so when I work with the directions I call in north as fire and south as earth, although you can keep the traditional northern hemisphere directions.

Here is an example of casting a circle and calling in the quarters using the traditional directions. Follow the steps in the "Before starting spell work" section (see page 10). Working in a clockwise direction:

- Face north and say: "I call in the energy of earth, of grounding and stillness."
- Turn to the east and say: "I call in the energy of air, of new life and awakening."
- Turn to the south and say: "I call in the energy of fire, of change and action."
- Turn to the west and say: "I call in the energy of water, of wisdom and emotion."
- Turn back to north and say: "The circle is cast. Only good must enter, any energy with ill intent must leave now! And so it is."
- Once you have performed your spell, say: "I thank the elements of earth, air, fire, and water for their assistance in making magick, this circle is now closed."

Angostura Bitters

I banish self-defeating thoughts and focus on my strengths.

Scientific name

Gentiana lutea

Healing properties

Often used in cocktails, Angostura Bitters is said to settle your stomach and aid the digestion of rich food.

MAGICKAL USES

Angostura Bitters can be used in spells to release or banish negative energies. It was once colloquially known as the magick potion because of its effectiveness in stopping nausea and is therefore associated with the solar plexus chakra. Angostura Bitters' primary ingredient is gentian root, giving the elixir its bitter, healing properties. Gentian root is traditionally used in spells to break hexes and curses.

Angostura repelling shot

This spell is for sending away negative self-talk.

The Angostura Bitters in this recipe will act as a cleansing agent to clear away damaging self-talk from your throat chakra.

INGREDIENTS

¾ fl oz | 25 ml water • 1 shot glass • 13 drops of Angostura Bitters

METHOD

Add the water to the shot glass and top with the Angostura Bitters.

Stand over a sink and swirl the potion in your mouth but *do not drink the potion:* forcefully spit it out, imagining you are spitting out all your discouraging words. It may take two or three goes. Once you have released all the liquid say: "I send all negative self-talk away; it has no power over me today."

Clap your hands three times to send it on its way.

JOURNAL

Once you have performed the spell affix the angostura potion sticker in the circle, affirming: "So mote it be."

Clove

My living space is clear, cleansed, and filled with light.

Scientific name

Eugenia caryophyllata

Healing properties

Clove oil is well known for reducing pain because of its analgesic properties. It also has antiseptic and antifungal qualities.

MAGICKAL USES

The purifying and cleansing nature of clove makes it perfect for protection spells. It is associated with the throat chakra and can encourage you to truly feel your emotions, both good and bad. A simple bracelet can be made from cotton and cloves, and when given to a friend or lover can help encourage a communicative and supportive relationship. Place three clove buds in your wallet or purse to attract wealth.

Clove purify your home mist

This spell is for giving your living space a physical and energetic cleanse.

All the oils in this mixture smell beautiful and are known for their anti-bacterial and anti-viral properties.

INGREDIENTS

2 drops of clove oil • 2 drops of lemon oil • 2 drops of petitgrain oil • 1 drop of cinnamon oil • 1 drop of rosemary oil • 1 drop of ylang ylang oil • 1 drop of lavender oil • ⅓ fl oz | 10 ml vodka (stops the oils from spoiling and does not affect the smell) • 1⅔ fl oz | 50 ml spray bottle • 1 fl oz | 35 ml distilled water • 1 clove sticker

METHOD

Place the oils and vodka into the spray bottle and top with the distilled water. Affix the clove sticker to the front of the bottle.

Liberally spray the mist around your home to purify the atmosphere. Wipe down surfaces, handles, and door knobs for a physical and energetic cleanse of your living space.

As you work affirm:
"My living space is clear, cleansed, and filled with light."

JOURNAL

Once you have performed the spell affix the clove potion sticker in the circle, affirming: "So mote it be."

Licorice

I take back control by setting healthy boundaries and saying "No."

Scientific name

Glycyrrhiza glabra

Healing properties

Licorice in the form of a lozenge can help soothe a sore throat and coughs. It is an excellent anti-viral and anti-bacterial.

MAGICKAL USES

Licorice opens your throat chakra so you can express yourself clearly and openly. Traditionally, licorice root has been used in spells to boost personal power and protection from those who wish you ill. The energy of licorice has a very commanding and strong presence: you could add a little of the dried powdered root to all spells to add more potency to them!

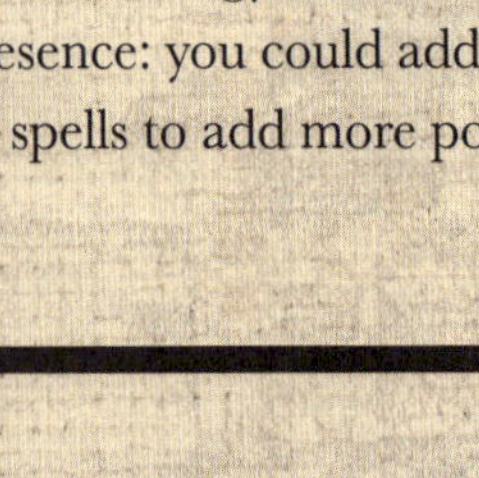

Licorice boundaries spell

This spell is for setting and keeping strong personal boundaries.

When you create a physical boundary around your name with licorice you also create etheric boundaries to keep your energy safe and strong.

INGREDIENTS

4–8 lengths of black licorice • 1 small plate • a pen • a piece of paper • 1 tsp salt • 1 tealight candle

METHOD

Arrange the licorice lengths on the plate to form a square box shape. Write your name on the paper and place it in the middle of the square, then add the salt and the candle.

As you light the candle say: "My personal boundaries are safe and strong. I take back control by saying 'No' when I need to. I am loyal to myself by choosing what I will and will not accept. So mote it be."

As the candle burns imagine a huge violet flame surrounding you, where any ill intent or people who take advantage of your good nature are repelled by the light.

Dispose of all the items once the candle is spent.

JOURNAL

Once you have performed the spell affix the licorice potion sticker in the circle, affirming: "So mote it be."

Sage

I am protected by a beautiful shield of white light.

Scientific name

Salvia officinalis

Healing properties

Sage has anti-bacterial and anti-viral properties, making it an excellent shield against illness. It is especially good for oral hygiene.

MAGICKAL USES

Sage is a well-known spiritual cleanser and clears any space of old and stale energies. Sage smoke purifies the atmosphere in a very physical sense as well, because it neutralizes bacteria. Associated with the third eye chakra, sage can open your mind to new possibilities and ways of living. The first thing you should do before you move into a new home is to sage all the rooms in the house!

Sage shielding spell

This spell is for getting rid of any unwanted or stale energy in your home.

Sage and salt are used in this spell to bless the water and fill it with light so it may bring brightness to your house. You will work with the cardinal directions to create a bubble of light around the area.

INGREDIENTS

a compass • 11 sage leaves • 1 tbs salt • a small clear quartz crystal • a small bowl of water • a wooden spoon

METHOD

Using the compass, work out where north, east, south, and west are in your living space. If your home has multiple levels, do this for each floor.

Place the sage, salt, and crystal into the bowl of water, and as you stir say:

"North, west, south, and east
All who enter this house
In body and in spirit
Do so with the highest intentions
That which does not bring my highest good
Must leave this place now."

Walk in a clockwise direction around the house and sprinkle the blessed water in the north, east, south, and west areas of your home, imagining each area filling with a beautiful protective shield of white light and forming a circle of protection around your home.

Place the crystal at the entrance of your home and pour the rest into the garden.

JOURNAL

Once you have performed the spell affix the sage potion sticker in the circle, affirming: "So mote it be."

Finding joy

Celeriac merry-making elixir

Dandelion hopes and wishes spell

Hyssop eloquence incantation

Lotus bento box

Peach creatrix zone

How finding joy spells work

Finding joy is all about doing what makes you happy more often. It seems so simple; however, we lead busy lives with many roles and responsibilities and it can be hard to find time for joy. If you can start off by finding five minutes each day to do something that makes your heart happy and then build up to an hour three times a week, you will find that these pockets of joy set up an energetic resonance to bring more joy into your energy body.

If you love doing something such as gardening, cooking, meditating, drawing, or any type of sporting activity, this will give you a clue about where you are meant to put your focus. Give yourself the gift of time and allow yourself to do activities that bring you joy every day, and you will see your life becoming more joyful over time. One of the delightful – or annoying – laws of the universe is that you create whatever you give your attention to. If you give your attention to always being busy and always working you will get more of this, but if you give your attention to finding more joy in your life then you will find more joy. The first step is to be aware of what makes you happy, because this may have been lost in the general shoulds and have-to's of everyday life.

I've been on the spiritual path for almost 40 years now, both in the Christian religion and witchcraft, and one of my observations is that there was not much room for humor in either one until recently. I was told many times to stop being so disrespectful when I was laughing with friends at church gatherings. With witchcraft, I used to tie myself in knots trying to get complicated spells and rituals right. There used to be a lot of gatekeeping as well, in that some people believed you could only be a real witch if you were born into a lineage and/or went through a rigorous initiation with a coven. Spiritual people tend to take themselves very seriously sometimes, including me, and forget to play and be silly.

People who allow themselves gentle self-care and grace when things go wrong usually have a healthy sense of humor and a great perspective on life. They are childlike, still curious about the world, and love to play, even well into their 80s and 90s. Be willing to be spontaneous and hold space for others to just be themselves, because this will bring a real sense of joy and connection.

The fun and simple spells in this section are designed to focus your mind back on joy and whimsy. You can even create them with others to form a joyful group energy: from making a magickal soup to share with friends to focusing on clarity and creativity, and even a legendary quest to go on! Make time in your life just for fun without the need to be productive, fulfill obligations, or earn money, and see how joy finds you more often.

Celeriac

I attract laughter, fun, and frivolity.

Scientific name

Apium graveolens var. *rapaceum*

Healing properties

Celeriac is an anti-diuretic that is often used for kidney health and can reduce inflammation. It may also improve heart health.

MAGICKAL USES

Celeriac will bring a burst of positive energy to all your spells. According to folklore it is has been used in sachets for love spells, and has been known to enhance psychic powers. It is associated with the third eye chakra. In metaphysical terms it is said to bring a purifying and balancing energy.

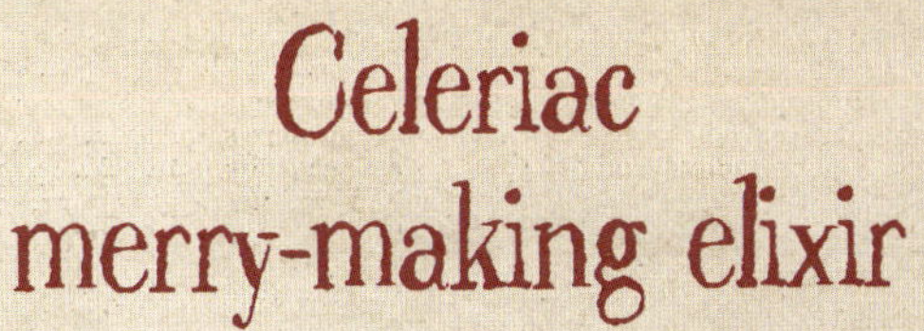Celeriac merry-making elixir

This spell is for happy parties and bringing people together over delicious food.

This soup is best made the day before serving. It makes a beautiful starter when served in fancy tea cups, topped with edible gold leaf and with fresh bread on the side.

INGREDIENTS

1 leek, chopped • 2 sticks of celery, chopped • 1 tbs olive oil • 1 oz | 30 g butter • salt and black pepper, to taste • 8¾ oz | 250 g cauliflower, chopped • 8¾ oz | 250 g celeriac, peeled and chopped • 1 tbs truffle oil • 17 fl oz | 500 ml full cream milk • 17 fl oz | 500 ml water • 1 vegetable stock cube • 5 fl oz | 150 ml pouring cream • edible gold leaf and fresh bread, optional

METHOD

Gently fry the leek and celery in a large saucepan in the oil and butter until the vegetables are softened and glossy. Add salt and pepper to taste and set aside.

Place the cauliflower and celeriac in a food processor and grind until fine. Add to a saucepan along with the truffle oil and fry gently for 2 to 3 minutes.

Add the leek and celery mix, milk, water, and stock cube and cook on medium heat, bloop, bloop, for about 20 minutes or until the soup loses it raw taste. Check for seasoning and adjust accordingly.

Cool in the fridge overnight, then puree the soup until it is of a velvety consistency. Gently reheat, then add the cream and stir through until combined. Just before serving, top with edible gold leaf and extra truffle oil if desired and serve with fresh, crusty bread.

JOURNAL

Once you have performed the spell affix the celeriac potion sticker in the circle, affirming, "So mote it be."

Dandelion

I release the past, I enjoy the present, and I look forward to the future.

Scientific name

Taraxacum spp.

Healing properties

The root and leaves of dandelion are used in tonics to improve liver and gall bladder health. The stem's white sap is said to be an excellent cure for warts.

MAGICKAL USES

The dandelion's puffy white flowers have long been associated with wishes granted when the seeds are blown into the wind. Allied with the third eye chakra, dandelion roots and leaves can be prepared and consumed in rituals designed to contact the spirit realm and enhance psychic abilities. Dandelion energy can be used in goal setting and manifestation.

Dandelion hopes and wishes spell

This spell is for the past, the present and the future.

Write down three hopes or wishes: one for the past, one for the present and one for the future. Decorate each frame with a dandelion sticker.

JOURNAL

Once you have performed the spell affix the dandelion potion sticker in the circle, affirming: "So mote it be."

Hyssop

I speak my truth clearly, and from the heart.

Scientific name

Hyssopus officinalis

Healing properties

The delicate, minty flavour of hyssop is very good for soothing sore throats and coughs. A tincture may help reduce blood pressure.

MAGICKAL USES

The hyssop plant's energy works on your throat chakra and is excellent for spells that involve unblocking this area. Hyssop resonates with your emotional body on an energetic level and brings unhealed emotions to the surface ready to be released. It is said that the fragrance of hyssop is connected with the angelic realm. Hyssop is used in purification and releasing spells.

Hyssop eloquence incantation

This spell is for clearing your throat chakra and helping you speak your truth.

Both the hyssop and chanting will work on your throat chakra to open it and bring healing to the area. Don't be surprised if you start coughing during this spell, as you will be releasing some of the energy blocks.

INGREDIENTS

favourite teacup • 6⅔ fl oz | 200 ml boiling water • 1 tsp dried hyssop leaves • honey, to taste

METHOD

Make yourself a cup of hyssop tea by pouring the boiling water over the leaves and steeping for 5 minutes.

Strain the liquid into your teacup and add honey to taste. Enjoy the tea, picturing the herb working its magic on your throat chakra.

Affirm: "I speak my truth clearly, and from the heart."

Start a sat nam chant (you will be easily able to find one on YouTube) and chant for 3 minutes. *Sat nam* means "Truth is my identity." It is a seed mantra from the kundalini yoga tradition that is said to open your throat chakra and help you speak your truth.

JOURNAL
Once you have performed the spell affix the hyssop potion sticker in the circle, affirming: "So mote it be.

Lotus

I am a limitless soul, enjoying a human experience.

Scientific name

Nelumbo nucifera

Healing properties

Lotus roots, seeds, stems, and flowers are all edible, and are said to promote longevity. Lotus root flour is gluten free.

MAGICKAL USES

The lotus flower has been a symbol of higher consciousness for thousands of years, according to the Buddhist and Hindu religions. As such it is associated with the crown chakra at the top of your head. This chakra is said to resemble a lotus flower with 1,000 petals, each petal unfolding as you reach new levels of enlightenment. The lotus flower symbolizes beauty, purity, and harmony.

Lotus bento box

This spell is for fun! Let's go on a legendary lotus quest . . .

It is not the destination but the journey that matters. Lotus bento box is a magickal scavenger hunt to foster joy, patience, and your powers of observation. Find nine different lotus items, with a lotus sticker provided to start you off. Look for photos, bookmarks, pressed lotus petals, tiny artworks: anything! Cut to size and place each in a square of the lotus bento box. Mark the date and location to form a memory collage of your quest.

BENTO BOX

JOURNAL

Once you have performed the spell affix the lotus potion sticker in the circle, affirming: "So mote it be."

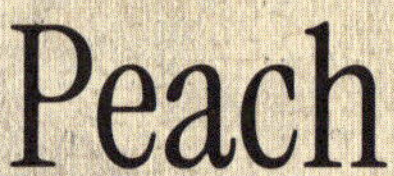

Peach

I am a brilliant and creative being.

Scientific name

Prunus persica

Healing properties

When peach leaves are boiled they create a medicine that has diuretic, laxative, and detoxifying properties.

MAGICKAL USES

The fragrant peach is excellent for spells that bring beauty and a sense of luxury to a space. They have also been associated with luck and longevity. Wood from the peach tree can make excellent divining rods, sticks with two points that can be used to find water, treasure, or buried objects. The stone of the peach can be dried and then carved with magickal inscriptions and worn to bring luck or protection.

Peach creatrix zone

This spell is for creating a magickal space for creative pursuits.

The peach brings its beautiful energy to your creative space, allowing for fresh insights.

INGREDIENTS

1 whole peach • 1 small birthday candle

METHOD

Carve a small section into the peach to fit the birthday candle; the peach effectively becomes a candle holder.

Light the candle and imagine a beautiful peach-colored light filling your office or studio space. This golden light is creating a magickal space so you can do your finest creative work in this peach creatrix zone.

Affirm to yourself that you are a brilliant and imaginative being who can bring joy to others through creative pursuits.

JOURNAL

Once you have performed the spell affix the peach potion sticker in the circle, affirming: "So mote it be."

Spiritual renewal
Cacao sacred ritual potion
Lavender chakra harmonizer
Passionflower angelic enchantment
Sunflower spirit house

How spiritual renewal spells work

Spiritual renewal can sometimes mean embracing your hermit era. The spells in this section are ones of self-reflection and solitude, of finding that quiet place within yourself that knows what the next step is. You just need to get quiet and ask. These spells can help you focus on your life purpose and bring a sense of balance and calm, while the rituals can be a part of your ultimate self-care tool kit.

Giving yourself time to seek peace and clarity can help you live a more peaceful and balanced life. The first step is to remember that you are a soul living on earth in a human body and having a physical experience. It has been likened to a roller-coaster ride in an amusement park, full of ups and downs and with moments of exhilarating joy and sheer terror. Knowing this can help you enjoy the good times with gratitude and weather the bad times with grace and understanding.

As part of my personal spiritual practice I do this nine chakras exercise every night before I go to sleep to remind myself I am connected with the divine, and to bring some peace and balance back to my physical body after the rigors of the day:

- Take three deep, slow breaths.
- Imagine a line of light going from your heart down into the molten core of Mother Earth. Bring that energy up from the earth into your earth star chakra, about 12 in/30 cm below your feet. This light makes its way up your body in a golden thread into your root chakra, sacral chakra, and solar plexus chakra, and then rests in your heart chakra.
- Take three more deep breaths.

- Imagine a line of light going from your heart up into the glowing light of the divine realm, symbolized by a sun. Bring that energy down from the sun into your soul star chakra, about 12 in/30 cm above your head. This light makes its way down your body in a golden thread into your crown chakra, third eye chakra, and throat chakra, and then rests in your heart chakra.
- Ask your higher self: "What does my soul want me to know right now?"

There's a game you can play with your sprit guides called the sign game. After the above exercise you can ask your guides to show you a sign that they are with you and to acknowledge you. Either they will show you the sign by giving you a picture in your mind, or you can come up with one.

As an example, just recently I was going through a worrying time with a family member. I asked my spirit guides to send me a sign of a white feather to show me that everything was going to be okay. Within the space of a week I had seen a white feather at work, then another on a footpath, and then while driving home one day I had to slow down because there were about 300 snowy white birds swarming on the road. They were flying from tree to tree, drinking from puddles on the road, and feasting on bugs in the grassy banks. There were white feathers flying everywhere. I wanted white feathers, and I got them in spades!

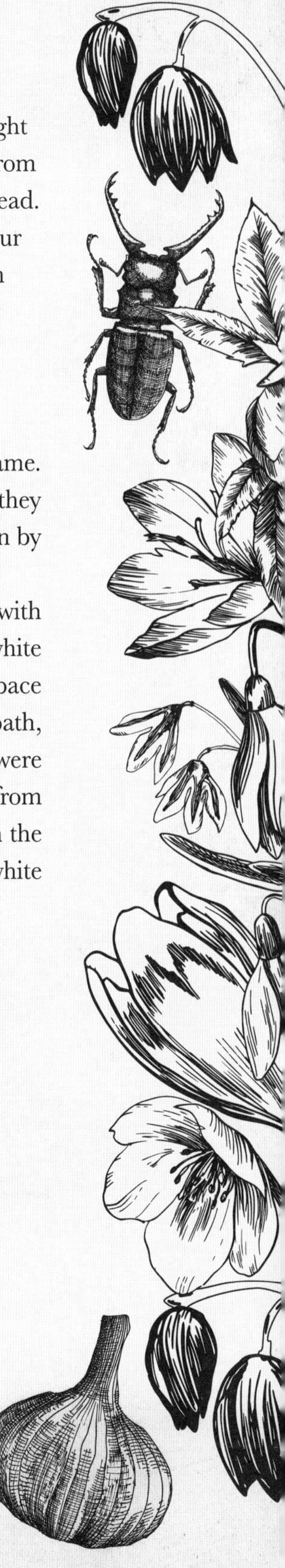

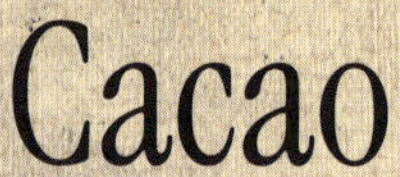

Cacao

I take the time for reflection and sacred ritual.

Scientific name

Theobroma cacao

Healing properties

Ingesting cacao can help increase the production of serotonin in your brain. It also has antioxidant properties.

MAGICKAL USES

Cacao is used in rituals to aid self-reflection and spiritual transformation. It is said that this plant can open your heart and lift your spirit to the higher realms, giving you access to sacred knowledge. For this reason it is associated with the heart chakra, for it can bring a feeling of oneness with the universe and all of humanity. As your heart chakra opens you can experience more empathy and connection with others.

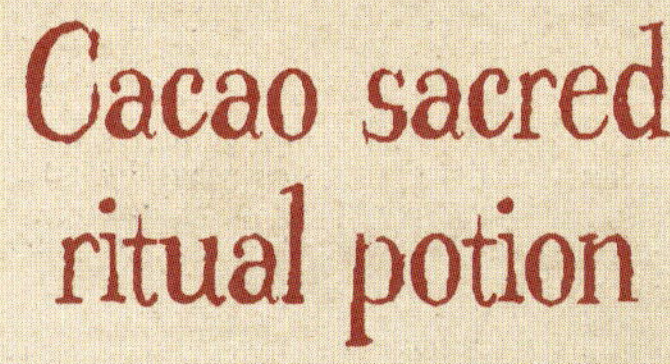

This spell is for contacting your higher self and discovering your soul purpose.

Cacao has been used in sacred ceremonies and rituals for thousands of years. Traditionally, it is the unroasted bean that is used, but for the purposes of this spell we will be using the easily accessible chocolate form of the cacao bean.

INGREDIENTS

8½ fl oz | 250 ml milk • 1 oz | 30 g 70 percent cocoa chocolate • dash of vanilla extract • grated nutmeg • 1 tsp honey or sugar

METHOD

Place all of the ingredients in a saucepan and stir over low heat until the chocolate is melted and mixed through.

As you mix, chant three times: "The highest light, brilliant bright, shine upon me tonight."

When the mixture has reached the desired temperature, pour it into your favourite mug. As you sip the potion, picture a gentle purple light surrounding you. Focus on your third eye, and ask your guides and angels to be present.

Write down any insights gifted to you from your team in spirit on the journal page.

JOURNAL

Once you have performed the spell affix the cacao potion sticker in the circle, affirming: "So mote it be."

Lavender

Red, orange, yellow, green, blue, indigo, and violet, all my energy centres are in alignment.

Scientific name

Lavandula angustifolia

Healing properties

The scent of lavender helps to calm your nervous system, soothes headaches, and brings emotional peace.

MAGICKAL USES

Lavender is often used in protection spells and to bring balance to your mind and body. It is associated with the third eye chakra and can restore peace to a troubled mind. A drop of lavender rubbed into the nape of your neck before bedtime can stop nightmares. Lavender is a well-known purification herb, so when you change the bed add a couple of drops of lavender to the fresh sheets.

Lavender chakra harmonizer

This spell is for balancing your chakras.

Chakras are centres of light in your etheric body that process unseen energy such as emotions. Like any system, they need to be regularly cleared and cleansed.

INGREDIENTS

lavender essential oil • 7 chakra stickers

METHOD

Take three, long deep breaths.

Following the diagram on page 162, from the base chakra to the crown chakra, dab a drop of lavender essential oil on each chakra point on your body, stating for each one:

- "My base chakra is aligned and filled with red light."
- "My sacral chakra is aligned and filled with orange light."
- "My solar chakra is aligned and filled with yellow light."
- "My heart chakra is aligned and filled with green light."
- "My throat chakra is aligned and filled with blue light."
- "My third eye chakra is aligned and filled with indigo light."
- "My crown chakra is aligned and filled with violet light."

Place each sticker on the corresponding chakra on page 163 in the opposite direction – from head to base – then say: "Violet, indigo, blue, green, yellow, orange, and red, all of my energy centres are in alignment."

JOURNAL
Write down how you felt
before and after harmonizing
your chakras.

CROWN CHAKRA
THIRD EYE CHAKRA
THROAT CHAKRA
HEART CHAKRA
SOLAR CHAKRA
SACRAL CHAKRA
BASE CHAKRA

Passionflower

When I ask my guides and angels for assistance, it is always given.

Scientific name

Passiflora incarnata

Healing properties

Passionflower is used in tonics and tinctures to help with insomnia and anxiety. Its mild sedative effect may help ease headaches.

MAGICKAL USES

Passionflower's magickal properties help you contact your higher self and spirit guides. Passionflower is associated with the opening of your crown chakra and being able to listen to guidance from your angels and team in spirit. This plant can even open up your channelling abilities and allows you to tap into guidance from the higher realms. Passionflower can help release fear and allow more divine light to flow into your crown chakra and down through your body.

Passionflower angelic enchantment

This spell is for solving a pressing problem.

Using a physical item you can touch such as a special rock can help bring your angelic helpers to the forefront of your mind.

INGREDIENTS

angelic wings sticker • a smooth, palm-sized rock • gloss varnish

METHOD

Affix the sticker to the rock and, if you wish, paint the sticker and rock with gloss varnish to preserve the wings.

This is now your special angel rock; every time you hold it you can ask your guides and angels for help with a problem you are having by saying: "When I ask my guides and angels for assistance it is always given. Show me a solution to this problem [name the problem]. Thank you, my team in spirit."

You may not hear the answer straight away, but trust that the perfect solution will arrive in time.

JOURNAL

Once you have performed the spell affix the passionflower potion sticker in the circle, affirming: "So mote it be."

Sunflower

I expand my light and lift my frequency.

Scientific name

Helianthus spp.

Healing properties

Eating sunflower seeds can improve your heart health and balance your blood sugar. A tincture may help reduce a fever.

MAGICKAL USES

The sunny energy of the sunflower brings strength and happiness. Sunflowers are, of course, connected with your sunny solar plexus chakra, which is responsible for confidence and a sense of personal power. The flower seeks the sun; thus it can teach you to seek joy, light, and the positive side of life. The sunflower can also represent or signify spiritual enlightenment.

Sunflower spirit house

This spell is for creating a safe and happy home.

A spirit house is a brightly colored little house much like a bird house displayed outside your home. This house honours the spirits of the land your home is built on, and hails from Buddhist teachings in South-east Asia. Offerings are made to keep the spirits happy. This spell builds on this concept by offering a gift to the spirits of the land near your home.

On a sunny day and with bare feet, sprinkle some sunflower seeds on the ground outside your home in a place you feel is special.

Feel the earth under your feet, breathe in the air, look up to the sky, and say:

"May the spirits of this land, bless my living space

May our house be filled with light and love

May I expand my light and lift my frequency

I honour the spirits of this land, thank you for keeping us safe and warm."

Know that your prayer of gratitude has been heard.

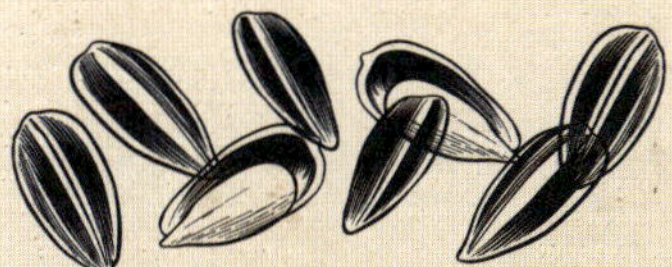

JOURNAL
Once you have performed the spell affix the sunflower potion sticker in the circle, affirming: "So mote it be."

Sticky situations
Black pepper banishing spell
Ginkgo clarity charm
Lemon aura cleanse
Olive peace vessel
Oregano return to me oil
Nutmeg psychic protection poppet

How sticky situations spells work

This section is full of spells to help you deal with people and situations that are being tricky or annoying. While you should never make the difficult person the bad guy, you can set up some good boundaries and practices that will help. In a way these are also protection spells with the added bonus of bringing in light to a situation to help heal it. There's even a spell to help you find lost objects!

I think sometimes we can get stuck in a bad-luck slump, and our thoughts start creating worse luck because this is where our focus is. Superstition can also play a big part in this, along with the power of suggestion. I believe negative thoughts can snowball if you give them enough attention, until suddenly you feel like you are a bad-luck magnet. Funnily enough, your firm belief in this can absolutely attract more bad luck, which is how frequency works: like attracts like. The best thing to do is break up stuck and stale energies by shaking yourself out of these thought patterns, and even seeking professional help if it's needed. Change that resonance and lift that frequency.

When I was 12 years old my mother received a curious free gift with a French cookbook subscription. It was a deck of mini tarot cards, and most of the images were less than positive. In fact, some of them were downright scary! My sister and I took turns to give each other readings, all of which ended in us shouting at each other: "OMG!! You're going to *die*!" Mum hid the cards from us and we never saw them again; however, the thought of those cards niggled at the edges of my mind. Were these cards cursed? Had they brought bad luck into the house? My assumption was based on the bad reputation tarot cards had at the time (this was the 1980s), and we were still of the mass mind that witchcraft and fortune telling was, at best, silly superstition and, at worst, downright evil. In hindsight, I believe that my thoughts about bad luck actually started attracting bad luck!

The truth is I did experiment with witchcraft and working with energy around this time, and the only books available to me were mostly to do with salacious hexes and curses. FYI, highly *not* recommended. In the 1980s there wasn't much information available on how to protect your energy, and for a little while I lived in fear. I dabbled with contacting the spirit world but, unfortunately, did not prepare myself properly and left my thoughts open to the kind of lower entities that thrive on anxious and worried minds. I did not know back then that there is a universal law: if you ask a spirit or an entity to leave they *must* leave. You make it very clear that they are not welcome, and you keep calling in your guides and angels to protect you.

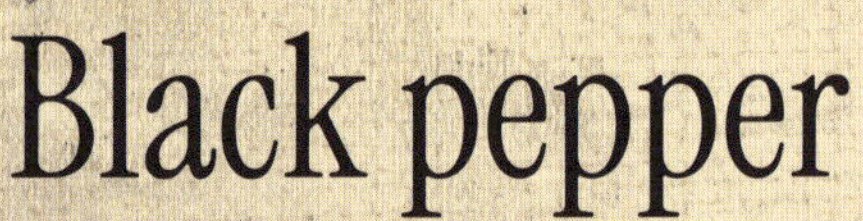

Black pepper

I send negative energy away.

Scientific name

Piper nigrum

Healing properties

Black pepper's warming qualities can reduce inflammation in your body and enhance circulation.

MAGICKAL USES

The spicy nature of black pepper makes it perfect for banishing spells. This plant is associated with the solar plexus chakra and can help dispel anger and frustration about your life circumstances. Certain limiting beliefs can be blasted away by the energy of black pepper, creating light and clarity.

Black pepper banishing spell

This spell is for when you have been feeling unlucky and things keep going wrong, as though you are stuck in a bad-luck rut.

This spell can dispel bad luck and bring in fresh energy.

INGREDIENTS

13 whole black peppercorns • splash of vinegar • 1 glass jar with a lid

METHOD

Place the peppercorns and vinegar in the jar, imagining if you wish that each peppercorn represents some negative energy. Pop the lid on the jar and shake it well. As you shake it chant three times: "Away from me, be gone! Unlucky luck, move on!"

Once you have done this you must throw the liquid out; that is, throw the spell down the sink as though you are throwing away all the bad luck. Imagine any negative energy being sent into the brilliant light of the sun to be transmuted.

JOURNAL

Once you have performed the spell affix the black pepper potion sticker in the circle, affirming: "So mote it be."

Ginkgo

I seek and speak clarity.

Scientific name

Ginkgo biloba

Healing properties

Ginkgo opens blood flow to your brain, improving memory and mental acuity. In pill form, it may help with mild dementia symptoms over time.

MAGICKAL USES

Ginkgo is said to bring vitality and good luck. This plant is associated with the crown chakra, as it connects your mind and body with the spirit. The herb physically brings clarity and, therefore, wisdom, and can be consumed whenever you need to make an important decision. The gingko is a sacred tree in some religions, connected with resilience and longevity.

Ginkgo clarity charm

This spell is for gaining insight into a confusing situation.

Automatic writing can be an excellent way to gain insights into a problem by asking your higher self to write through you. If you are seeking clarity about a situation that is confusing you, work your magick with this charm to gain some insights.

INGREDIENTS

3 tsp dried ginkgo leaves • 1 clear quartz crystal • a small draw string pouch • a notebook • 6⅔ fl oz | 200 ml boiled water • a pen

METHOD

Place 2 teaspoons of the ginkgo leaves and the crystal in the pouch and place the pouch beside the notebook.

Make a cup of ginkgo tea by steeping the remaining leaves in the boiled water for 5 minutes. As you enjoy the cup of tea, ask the ginkgo plant spirit to help you see this situation clearly.

Using the pen, start automatic writing in your journal. This means writing whatever comes into your mind without second-guessing it. Even if you get stuck you can keep writing the same word over and over until the flow begins.

Allow yourself to write for at least 5 minutes. You may be surprised by the insights gained that will help bring clarity to your situation.

Place the charm under your pillow and affirm that you will receive further insights in your dreams.

JOURNAL
Once you have performed the spell affix the gingko potion sticker in the circle, affirming: "So mote it be."

Lemon

My aura is golden and bright.

Scientific name

Citrus x *limon*

Healing properties

Lemon is an excellent anti-bacterial and anti-viral. Full of vitamin C, lemons are great for keeping your skin soft and clean.

MAGICKAL USES

Lemons are used in spells to clear away any unwanted or negative energy. They are associated with the throat chakra and can help you speak your truth, despite fears of self-judgment. Make a cut in a lemon, then write down a habit or feeling you want to get rid of on a small piece of paper. Place the paper inside the lemon and bury the lemon in the earth.

Lemon aura cleanse

This spell is for cleansing your aura of any energy blocks.

This scrub is best used in the bath or shower. A word to the wise: do not use it on your face or tender bits!

INGREDIENTS

1¾ oz | 50 g salt • zest and 2 tbs of juice from 1 lemon • 5 drops of lemon essential oil • 2 tsp calendula oil

METHOD

Mix all of the ingredients in a jar or bowl.

Using a soft body brush or flannel, gently scrub your torso, arms, and legs in a circular motion with the scrub. As you do so, imagine a golden light clearing away any energetic blocks and leaving your aura clean, clear, and lemony fresh.

Concentrate on areas that feel stagnant and ask for any energy that is not for your highest good to be sent away. Affirm that your aura is golden and bright.

Wash the scrub from your body with warm water. You will feel cleansed, both physically and energetically.

JOURNAL
Once you have performed the spell affix the lemon potion sticker in the circle, affirming: "So mote it be."

Olive

In the end, only love matters.

Scientific name

Olea europaea

Healing properties

Olives, especially olive oil, are great for supporting heart health because they are full of anti-oxidants.

MAGICKAL USES

Olives can be used in spells for peace and to heal arguments. This plant is associated with the heart chakra and symbolizes love and resilience. The olive branch as a symbol of peace ensures that olives used in spells for reconciliation and harmonious relationships will be successful. Olive oil can also be used in cleansing and purifying rituals.

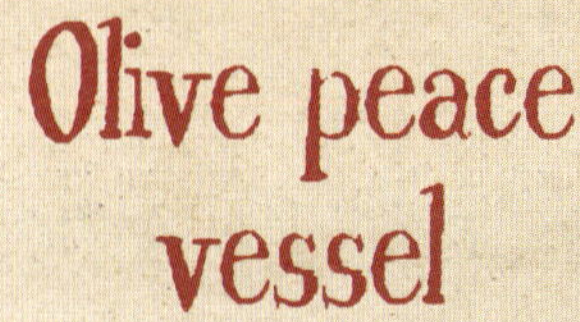

Olive peace vessel

This spell is for healing any rifts after a serious argument.

Only perform this spell if you are prepared to offer an olive branch to the person and start to heal the relationship.

INGREDIENTS

a toothpick • 2 olives • 2 bay leaves • 2 small sprigs of olive leaves, plus extra to decorate • olive oil • a small jar with a lid • 15½ in | 40 cm length of white ribbon • 1 olive sticker

METHOD

Using the toothpick, carve one olive with your initials and the other olive with the initials of the person with whom you have a rift.

Place the bay leaves, olive leaves, and carved olives into the jar and top with enough olive oil to cover. Secure tightly with the lid.

Affix the sticker to the front of the jar and tie the jar up with the ribbon. Attach some of the extra olive leaves. Leave the jar to do its work.

Send the person in question loving and peaceful thoughts without any expectation of anything in return. Once the relationship has been healed, discard the contents of the jar into the earth and give thanks.

JOURNAL

Once you have performed the spell affix the olive potion sticker in the circle, affirming: "So mote it be."

Oregano

That which has been lost
will now return to me.

Scientific name

Origanum vulgare

Healing properties

Oregano is a great anti-viral oil and natural antibiotic. It can be used as a disinfectant in soaps and sanitizers.

MAGICKAL USES

Oregano is useful in spells to find lost items or when seeking treasure to boost your luck. It is associated with the base chakra and is said to build your sense of power and resilience. It's a plant that can help you feel safe and that all is right in your world through its comforting spicy and herby aroma. According to folklore, oregano essential oil can make witches' warts disappear!

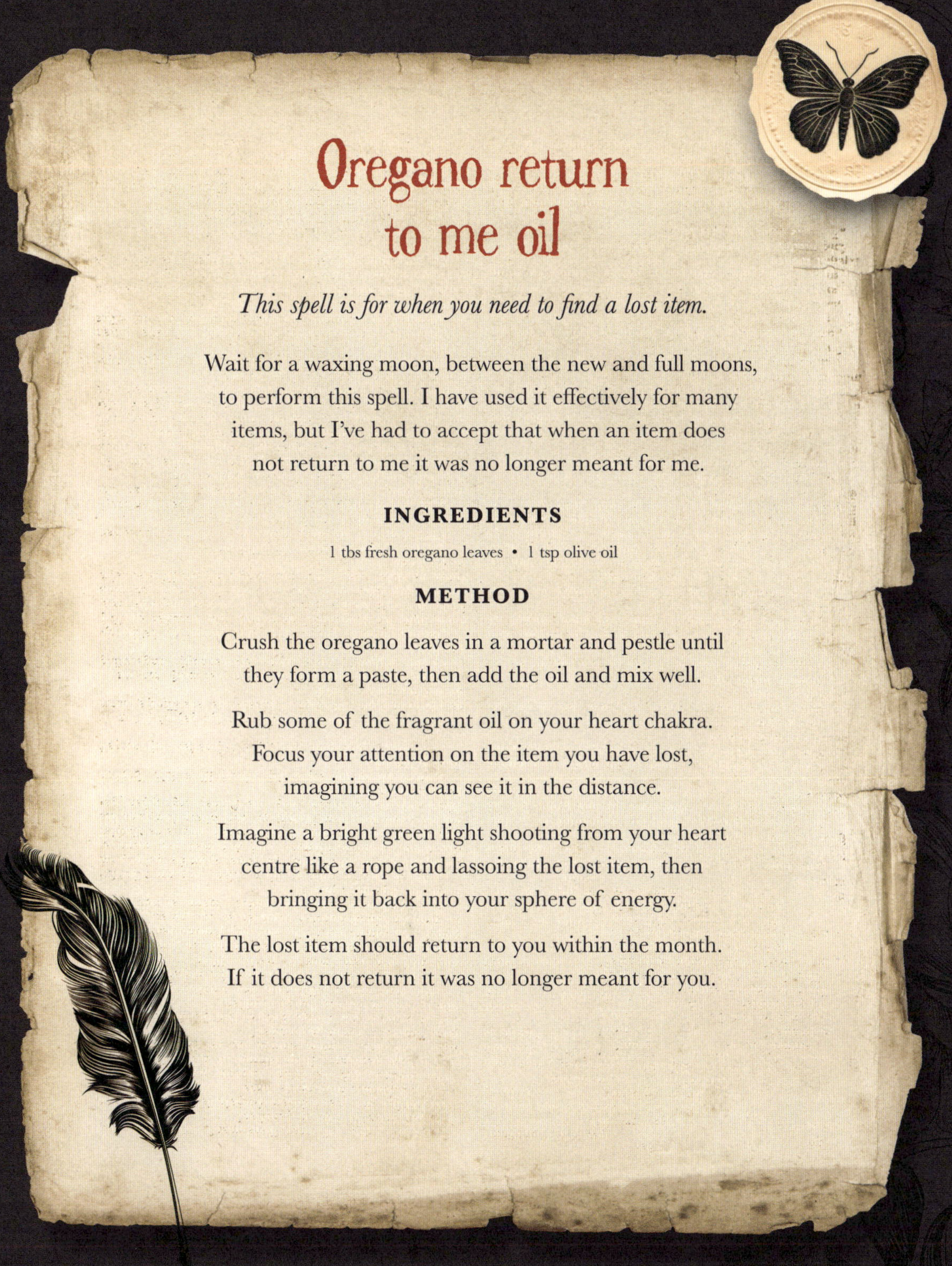

Oregano return to me oil

This spell is for when you need to find a lost item.

Wait for a waxing moon, between the new and full moons, to perform this spell. I have used it effectively for many items, but I've had to accept that when an item does not return to me it was no longer meant for me.

INGREDIENTS

1 tbs fresh oregano leaves • 1 tsp olive oil

METHOD

Crush the oregano leaves in a mortar and pestle until they form a paste, then add the oil and mix well.

Rub some of the fragrant oil on your heart chakra. Focus your attention on the item you have lost, imagining you can see it in the distance.

Imagine a bright green light shooting from your heart centre like a rope and lassoing the lost item, then bringing it back into your sphere of energy.

The lost item should return to you within the month. If it does not return it was no longer meant for you.

JOURNAL
Once you have performed the spell affix the oregano potion sticker in the circle, affirming: "So mote it be."

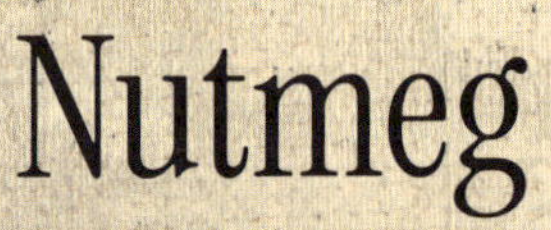

Nutmeg

I am protected from harm, always.

Scientific name

Myristica fragrans

Healing properties

Nutmeg is primarily used to aid digestion and can also help energize your body and improve your mood.

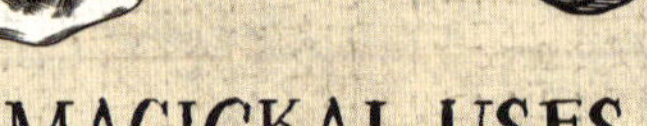

MAGICKAL USES

Nutmeg is excellent to use in money and protection spells, as its heady aroma is said to attract wealth and repel negative energies. Nutmeg is associated with the sacral chakra, as it is a known aphrodisiac and can help boost creativity. It also works on the third eye, by opening up your psychic powers. A whole nutmeg placed under the bed is said to support a long-lived, loyal relationship.

The power of poppets

The nutmeg psychic protection poppet is a powerful spell that is not to be taken lightly. That's why I have placed it at the end of this chapter. Poppets are little effigies created by the spell caster to bring about healing, love, or protection. They can also be known by the term "spirit doll." They are a container of energy. These dolls usually take on a human form or, at the very least, a personality. Poppets are designed to be a messenger or vessel for the creator's wishes, and some of these enchanted dolls have been found in tombs as far back as Ancient Egypt, made from cloth, wood, and human hair. There is a strong belief in many cultures that inanimate objects designed to look human contain power.

Poppets are often made from natural materials such as cloth, wood, clay, or metal, and they can be stuffed or decorated with rocks, crystals, seashells, or special talismans. Some poppets even have little spell scrolls wrapped around their arms or neck or wood carved with prayers placed inside them. Like any magick, poppets can be used for good or nefarious purposes. It is advised not to make a poppet to represent another person to work magick with, as this goes against a person's free will.

The following poppet spell is a powerful protection spell. It is a spirit doll created by you for your house to protect you from physical and/or psychic attack. It is a little effigy that will set up the resonance of protection in the area you display it in. You put your intent within the doll while you are creating it, and thus it becomes a container for your wishes. When creating this poppet call in the light of Archangel Michael to protect you and your loved ones, to help make your home safe and secure and to guard against nightmares.

Take as long as you need to create the poppet: it can be a little project you work on for days or weeks. Working with your hands will help set up the meditative state of mind needed to imbue the doll with shielding energy.

Nutmeg psychic protection poppet

This spell is for creating a protective poppet to keep your home safe from physical and psychic trespassers.

Poppets are an excellent way to store energetic intent, and they also look great when dotted around your home.

INGREDIENTS

3 whole nutmegs • poppet template (see page 203) • a piece of baking paper, A4 size • pins • 2 pieces of purple felt, A4 size, placed together • a needle • purple thread • fibre-fill stuffing • 1 small amethyst crystal • 7 drops of nutmeg essential oil • 1 small blue evil eye glass charm (nazar amulet*), or use the sticker • 19½ in | 50 cm length of purple ribbon • sage smudge stick or your favourite incense

METHOD

Grate the nutmegs slightly to release their fragrance.

Trace the outline of the poppet template on the baking paper and pin to the pieces of purple felt. Cut around the outline and discard the paper and felt scraps. You will have two purple poppet shapes.

Use the needle and purple thread to start sewing around the head of the poppet, but before you sew the neck area fill the head with some of the stuffing and the whole nutmegs.

Continue to sew the neck of the poppet and halfway down the body. When you reach the widest part, stuff with the remaining filling, the amethyst crystal, and the nutmeg oil.

Sew up the rest of the poppet until everything is joined.

Sew or stick on the nazar amulet as the eye of the poppet and tie the neck with the purple ribbon.

You can continue to decorate as you wish with found objects and pretties to make the poppet truly your own.

To consecrate your poppet, pass it through some sage smoke and state: "I am protected from harm, always."

Hang the poppet in your home in an area you feel that they belong. This poppet will act as a protective amulet to keep your home safe.

** The nazar symbol originated thousands of years ago in Sumer, a civilization that no longer exits, and was used by many cultures across the world to protect against harm.*

JOURNAL

Once you have performed the spell affix the nutmeg potion sticker on the poppet diagram, affirming: "So mote it be."

Bonus spell: archangel feather box 777

This spell is for inviting seven archangels into your home for seven days.

The angel number 777 signifies that you are on the right soul path and that divine luck is on your side. This spell builds on the concept of hosting the archangels, which was originally inspired by German medium Imiri. You will invite seven archangels into your home and host them for seven days, observing for miracles and divine inspiration during this time.

INGREDIENTS

7 white feathers • a small glass box with a lid,
approximately 8 in x 6 in | 20 cm x 15 cm • 1 white candle

METHOD

Choose a day you wish to start hosting the archangels. Place the seven feathers inside the feather box, naming each feather for an archangel by saying:

"From the east, Archangel Raphael for healing

From the south, Archangel Michael for protection

From the west, Archangel Gabriel for strength

From the north, Archangel Uriel for prosperity

From above, Archangel Metatron for guidance

From below, Archangel Sandalphon for wishes come true

From the heart, Archangel Chamuel for peace."

Close the lid and place the archangel feather box just inside the entrance of your home. Open the front door and say: "Dear archangels, welcome to my home!"

Light the candle to guide the archangels' way, and know that they will be present with you over the next seven days. Ideally the candle will be burning the whole time, so an LED candle may be best. Be sure to record any insights and guidance you receive during this special time.

At the end of the seven days open your front door and bid the archangels farewell, thanking them for their presence. You can continue to display the feather box in your house as a beautiful reminder that the angels will be with you whenever you need them.

JOURNAL

Once you have performed the archangel feather box 777 spell write down your observations.

Spell envelope

Make a note of your favourite spells and the dates you performed them by writing them down on separate pieces of paper and placing them in the envelope attached. In 12 months, open the envelope and see how many of your spells have been successful.

Spells are a form of manifestation and will only be successful if the results are for your highest good. I have performed many spells in the past that, with hindsight, I have been very grateful when they did not come to pass! The old adage "Be careful what you wish for" holds true.

Acknowledgments

A sincere thank you to you, reading this right now.

I read somewhere that the activity you most love when you are 10 years old is a clue to what your soul purpose is in this life. Mine was coloring, drawing, and creating books. In 1984 I wrote a hand-made book called "Witches' Magical Spells." The book consisted of loose-leaf felt-tip pen color illustrations on pieces of file paper, enclosed in a cardboard and paper cover. It had many dubious spells contained within such as "How to get a headache," "How to make a spider angry," and "How to become famous." I was so proud of it!

Even in my 20s I would take it out and read it and laugh at all the silly spells. It was extra special because it had fancy glitter stars stuck onto the cover with glue and pictures inside of potion bottles, black cats, and witches. The last time I saw it was in 1997, when I showed it as an artefact to our Full Moon Magick group. Now, sadly, it has been lost to the mists of time.

In a way that little book was the prototype for *Witch's Magickal Spellbook*, but I can assure you the spells are much more sophisticated now as I have had much spell practice through trial and error over the last 40 years! All the spells in this book have been tried and tested by me, and some are my favourite go-to's whenever I need help with a situation.

I would like to thank everyone who has bought and enjoyed this book. I hope it brings you much joy!

Bibliography

Brown, Mary Jane, 2018. *What is celeriac? A root vegetable with surprising benefits.* https://www.healthline.com/nutrition/celeriac.

Cavendish, Lucy, 2013. *Spellbound: The secret grimoire of Lucy Cavendish,* Rockpool Publishing, Sydney, Australia.

Cho, Richard W. et al., 2015. Phosphorylation of complexin by PKA regulates activity-dependent spontaneous neurotransmitter release and structural synaptic plasticity. *Neuron*, 88(4), 749–61.

Culpeper, Nicolas, 1983, *Culpepper's Colour Herbal*, W. Foulsham & Co. Ltd, Suffolk, UK.

Darcey, Cheralyn, 2017. *Flowerpaedia: 1000 flowers and their meanings*, Rockpool Publishing, Sydney, Australia.

Daniels, Estelle and Paul Tuitéan, 1998. *Pocket Guide to Wicca*, Crossing Press, California, USA.

De Pulford, Nicola, 1998. *The Book of Spells: Over 400 secret recipes to get your own way in love, work, and play*, Quarto Publishing, London, UK.

Farrer-Halls, Gill, 2009. *The aromatherapy bible: The definitive guide to using essential oils,* Godsfield Publishing, London, UK.

Gerber, M, 2021, *Sticker Studio Apothecary: A sticker gallery for modern mystics*, Castle Point Books, New York, USA.

Giesemann, Suzanne, 2024. *The Awakened Way: Making the shift to a divinely guided life,* Hay House LLC, California, USA.

Grayland-Leech, Bethany, 2025. Health benefits of gingko biloba, https://www.medicalnewstoday.com/articles/263105

Grieve, Mrs M., nd. Olive, https://www.botanical.com/botanical/mgmh/o/olive.

Grieve, Mrs M., nd. Sunflower, https://www.botanical.com/botanical/mgmh/s/sunflower.

Hardie, Titania, 2001. *White Magic: Titania's book of favorite spells*, Quadrille Publishing, London, UK.

Jakubczyk, Karolina et al, 2018. Garden nasturtium *(Tropaeolum majus L.)* – a source of mineral elements and bioactive compounds, Rocz Panstw Zakl Hig. 2018;69(2):119–126. PMID: 29766690.

Matthews, John, 2004. *The Sidhe: Wisdom from the Celtic otherworld*. The Lorian Press, Washington, USA.

McCoy, Edain, 1990. *Lady of the Night: A handbook of moon magick & rituals*, Llewellyn Publications, Minnesota, USA.

McCoy, Edain 1993, *Witta: An Irish Pagan tradition*, Llewellyn Publications, Minnesota, USA.

Nutrition Council of Australia, nd. 4 benefits of cacao for your health, https://nutritioncouncilaustralia.com.au/4-benefits-of-cacao-for-your-health/

paganpages.org, 2020. Notes from the Apothecary: Celery, https://paganpages.org/emagazine/2020/02/01/notes-from-the-apothecary-58/.

Psychic Lauryn, 2016. Host the Archangels at your Home!, https://www.psychiclauryn.com/post/2017/09/13/host-the-archangels-at-your-home.

Purchon, Nerys and Dhenu Jennifer Clary, 1990. *Herbcraft: The cultivation and use of herbs*, Hodder & Stoughton, Sydney, Australia.

Purchon, Nerys, 1998. *Nery's Purchon's Handbook of Natural Healing*, Allen & Unwin, Sydney, Australia.

Ravenwolf, Silver, 2002. *To Ride a Silver Broomstick: New generation witchcraft*, Llewellyn Publications, Minnesota, USA.

Ravenwolf, Silver, 2018. *Poppet Magick: Patterns, spells & formulas for poppets, spirit dolls & magickal animals*, Llewellyn Publications, Minnesota, USA.

Roman, Sanaya, 1992. *Spiritual Growth: Being your higher self*, New World Library, California, USA.

Roman, Senaya, 2007. *Creating Money: Attracting Abundance*, New World Library, California, USA.

Roman, Sanaya, 2011. *Living with Joy: Keys to personal power & spiritual transformation*, New World Library, California, USA.

Stewart, Amy, 2013. *The Drunken Botanist: The plants that create the world's great drinks*, Timber Press, Oregon, USA.

Stewart, Amy, 2010. *Wicked Plants: The weed that killed Lincoln's mother and other botanical atrocities*, Timber Press, Oregon, USA.

Stinson, Adrienne, 2023. Benefits of passionflower for anxiety and insomnia, https://www.medicalnewstoday.com/articles/323795.

Tinderbox, 2019. *Essential oil companion: Aromatherapy wisdom for the spiritual being being human*, Tinderbox, Perth, Australia.

Trafton, Anne, 2015. Neuroscientists reveal how the brain can enhance connections, http://news.mit.edu/2015/brain-strengthen-connections-between-neurons-1118.

Wauters, Ambika, 2002. *The book of chakras: Discover the hidden forces within you*, Quarto Publishing, London, UK.

Worwood, Valerie Ann, 1998, *The fragrant heavens: The spiritual dimension of fragrance and aromatherapy*, Cox & Wyman Ltd, London, UK.

About the author

Priestess Moon's books and oracle cards are divination tools designed to help you access your intuition. She paints magickal energy into the artworks and writes the guidebooks based on life experiences, metaphysical concepts, and extensive research. Using the cards will support you in answering questions, reassure you, and bring solace.

Priestess Moon is the author of *Enchanted Spell Oracle, Making Magick, Making Magick Oracle, Enchanted Unicorn Oracle, Deadly Apothecary Oracle,* and *Medieval Herb Sigils*. Her oracle decks come from the heart and are created with the wish that they bring you joy, delight, and magick!

priestessmoondesign.com

priestessmoondesign

priestess.moon99

priestessmoondesign

GOLDEN
TICKET

SAFFRON
TOMATO
ARNICA
CARAWAY
CRANBERRY
ROSEMARY
BASIL
ANGOSTURA
VANILLA
VANILLA
BLACK PEPPER
CELERY
CELERY
GINSENG
PLUM

SAGE
CELERIAC
DANDELION
CLOVE
CLOVE
HYSSOP
LOTUS
LOTUS
PEACH
GINGER
CACAO
LAVENDER
PASSION FLOWER
PASSION FLOWER
BLACK PEPPER
GINKGO
LEMON
ALFALFA
NUTMEG
OLIVE
OLIVE
OREGANO
ALFALFA